Fodor's InFocus

ST. MAARTEN/ ST. MARTIN, ST. BARTH, AND ANGUILLA

Welcome to St. Maarten/St. Martin, St. Barth, and Anguilla

St. Maarten/St. Martin, St. Barth, and Anguilla, a string of Caribbean islands in the Lesser Antilles, are proof good things come in threes. Their proximity and frequent connections make it a breeze to hop from paradise to paradise, from the posh villas of St. Barth to "Restaurant Row" in St. Martin to the picture-perfect beaches of Anguilla. While each island has its own personality, you can't go wrong with any, especially if you're looking for a sun-drenched vacation with your toes in the sand.

TOP REASONS TO GO

★ **Brilliant Beaches:** From Shoal Bay to Simpson Bay Beach, the beaches are legendary.

★ **Fine Dining:** Dinner with a sea view is especially great in St. Martin.

★ **Dreamy Resorts:** You won't lift a finger at the hotels here.

★ **Shopping:** Indulge at duty-free stores in Philipsburg and luxury boutiques in St. Barth.

★ **Cultural Mix:** The islands offer a unique mix of French, Dutch, and Caribbean lifestyles.

★ **Adventure:** Go zip-lining, horseback riding, kayaking, and snorkeling.

Contents

MAPS

Chapter 1

EXPERIENCE ST. MAARTEN/ ST. MARTIN, ST. BARTH, AND ANGUILLA

16 ULTIMATE EXPERIENCES

St. Maarten/St. Martin, St. Barth, and Anguilla offer terrific experiences that should be on every traveler's list. Here are Fodor's top picks for a memorable trip.

1 Shoal Bay, Anguilla

This 2-mile-long beach has powdery-soft sand and breathtaking turquoise water, making it one of the best of many beautiful beaches on the tiny island of Anguilla. *(Ch. 5)*

2 Loterie Farm, St. Martin

Zipline or hike at this family-friendly nature reserve and you'll be rewarded with views of Pic Paradis, the highest mountain on the island. Then, relax at the farm's cabana-lined pool. *(Ch. 3)*

3 Shopping, St. Barth

Even if you're just window-shopping, St. Barth is the Caribbean's ultimate destination for brand names and high-end boutiques, especially on Quai de la Republique in Gustavia. *(Ch. 4)*

4 Lunch at the Lolos, St. Martin

Some of the best dining bargains (and barbecue) in St. Martin can be found at outdoor roadside grills in Grand Case, the French side's culinary capital. *(Ch. 3)*

5 Elvis's Beach Bar, Anguilla

You can have one of the best rum punches in the Caribbean at this bar, which was made from a beached boat. Nothing beats being here with your feet in the sand during sunset. *(Ch. 5)*

6 Marigot, St. Martin

Don't miss the bustling harbor, streetside cafés, and boutiques of St. Martin's lovely seaside French capital. *(Ch. 3)*

7 Junior's Glass Bottom Boat, Anguilla

Junior Fleming and his glass-bottom boat are a bona fide Anguilla institution. The glass bottom is perfect for watching sea life without getting wet but you can also jump in and snorkel. *(Ch. 5)*

8 Golf at Aurora, Anguilla

A must for any serious golfer, this 18-hole course designed by Greg Norman has amazing views, with 13 out of 18 holes right on the water. *(Ch. 5)*

9 Ziplining in St. Maarten

Fly high over the Dutch side with the steepest vertical drop in the world at Rainforest Adventures. *(Ch. 3)*

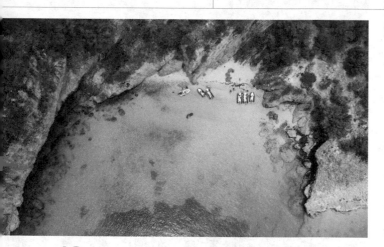

10 Little Bay, Anguilla

Jump off "the Rock" at Little Bay beach, accessible only by boat or by scampering down a rope to the beach from the hill. There are two hills, one a bit taller than the other. *(Ch. 5)*

11 Maho Beach, St. Maarten

Watching planes land ridiculously low over your head at Maho Beach
(or watching the people watching the planes) is one of the most
popular activities in Dutch St. Maarten. *(Ch. 3)*

12 Baie Orientale, St. Martin

With trendy beach clubs and restaurants, this beach is a vibrant scene.
The southern end of the beach is clothing-optional. *(Ch. 3)*

13 Dune Preserve, Anguilla

Caribbean reggae artist Bankie Banx created this unforgettable musical oasis not far from the Aurora Resort. Order a bite to eat and relax with your toes in the sand. *(Ch. 5)*

14 Anse de Grande Saline, St. Barth

Pounding surf, undeveloped shoreline, and an absence of facilities make this pristine beach feel wild, in the best way. Its seclusion makes it a natural choice for nudists. *(Ch. 4)*

15 Hotel Le Toiny Restaurant, St. Barth

Located high above Anse Toiny on St. Barth's Southeastern coast, the Hotel Le Toiny Restaurant is one of the island's premier dining destinations. The view is one of the best on the island. *(Ch. 4)*

16 Sundown in Philipsburg, St. Maarten

After a long day of duty-free shopping and lounging on the beach, grab a drink and watch the colors change over this bustling port. *(Ch. 3)*

WHAT'S WHERE

1 St. Maarten/St. Martin.
Two nations (Dutch and
French), many nationalities,
one small island, a lot of development. But there are also
more white, sandy beaches
than days in a month. Go for
the awesome restaurants,
extensive shopping, and wide
range of activities. Don't go if
you're not willing to get out
and search for the really good
stuff.

2 St. Barthélemy. If you come
to St. Barth for a taste of
European village life, not for a
conventional full-service
resort experience, you will be
richly rewarded. Go for excellent dining and wine, great
boutiques with the latest hip
fashions, world-class
people-watching, and an
active, on-the-go vacation.
Don't go for big resorts, and
make sure your credit card is
platinum-plated.

3 Anguilla. With miles of
brilliant white sand and
accommodations that range
from funky guesthouses to
elegant super-luxury resorts,
Anguilla is a laid-back beach
lover's heaven. Go for fine
cuisine in elegant surroundings, great snorkeling,
family-friendliness, and the
funky late-night music scene.
This island is all about relaxing and reviving. Don't go for
shopping and sightseeing.

Scrub
Island

The Bahamas

ATLANTIC OCEAN

Cuba

Dominican
Republic

Haiti

Jamaica

Puerto
Rico

Caribbean Sea

COLOMBIA   VENEZUELA

ATLANTIC OCEAN

Colombier   Lorient   Anse de
                                    Petit Cul de Sac

GUSTAVIA   Lurin   **2**

St. Barthélemy

0   5 mi

0   5 km

Anguilla's Best Beaches

ISLAND HARBOUR
Located on Northeast Anguilla, Island Harbour is primarily a fishing village but there's a tranquil little beach, too. There are laid-back beach restaurants, and it's a great place to meet locals.

SANDY GROUND
For buzzy nightlife, Sandy Ground is where everyone in Anguilla seems to end up. It's home to several open-air bars and restaurants, boat-rental operations, the ferry to Sandy Island—and frequent parties.

LITTLE BAY
This gray-sand beach is often referred to as "Little Anguilla Beach at Little Bay" and yes, it's quite little. It's also quiet, ultra-relaxing, and only plays host to a few beachgoers at any given time. And, if you like snorkeling, night dives, or climbing rocks and jumping off the top into the water, this is the spot. You must get here either by climbing down a rock ledge using ropes or by boat from Crocus Bay.

MEADS BAY
Gorgeous Meads Bay stands out because of its top resorts and fine restaurants. Stay at dreamy places like Malliouhana and Carimar Beach Club. The powder-soft champagne sand is great for a long walk.

MAUNDAYS BAY
This scenic crescent-shaped beach is great for swimming and long beach walks. It's the home of Belmond Cap Juluca, one of the island's most posh resorts, which is located along the shore.

Shoal Bay

SHOAL BAY

It's a beach so nice they named it twice: Shoal Bay East and Shoal Bay West. The one most everyone refers to is Shoal Bay East. Possibly the single most photographed of Anguilla's beaches, Shoal Bay has powder-fine slightly pinkish sand, near-constant light tradewinds, that only-in-the-Caribbean turquoise water, and the spectrum of services that spells the difference between a perfect beach and one that's perfectly extraordinary.

RENDEZVOUS BAY

With its dazzling blue water, Rendezvous Bay is a fitting home of the beautiful CuisinArt Golf Resort and Spa as well as Bankie Banx's famous beach bar, the Dune Preserve. It's a long-time favorite of many island visitors because of its striking beauty and pristine sand.

CAPTAIN'S BAY

Although you may have heard of Captain's Bay, chances are you haven't gone there. Located near the somewhat distant East End of Anguilla, Captain's Bay is not easy to get to: you need to know exactly where you're going (an experienced local guide can help). While there are no signs and no services, you're rewarded with beauty and privacy.

SANDY ISLAND

The small but gorgeous beach at this offshore cay delivers true serenity. It's well worth the ferry trip from Sandy Ground.

Best Restaurants in St. Maarten/St. Martin

SPIGA

At this Italian restaurant, quality ingredients are sourced from around the world, and the result is one of the most spectacular menus in the Caribbean. It's located in a beautifully restored old Creole home in Grand Case.

MARIO BISTROT

Located in the Mediterranean-style village of Porto Cupecoy, Mario's eclectic French menu items with a strong Caribbean influence have been delighting visitors for more than 25 years. Whether you seek fine aged beef or the freshest of seafood, don't forget that you must, somehow, leave room for dessert.

IZI RISTORANTE ITALIANO

This upbeat Simpson Bay restaurant is nonstop fun on the surface, but the chef is all business in the kitchen. His insistence on top-notch ingredients has paid off in loyal clients and lots of awards, including best Italian restaurant. Try the tasting menu with outstanding wines, by reservation only.

LA CIGALE

The views of the lagoon from this upscale French restaurant near Marigot are almost as wonderful as the dining experience. From the excellent service to the artistic dish presentation, you'll savor this one well after your vacation is over.

VESNA TAVERNA

Located in Simpson Bay, Vesna's Greek-French fusion is always a favorite. The owners scour the world for new recipes for their evening specials. The restaurant has full American breakfast (try the homemade bagel tower with lox and egg), lunch, and dinner, but the best is Saturday for Greek Night.

SKIPJACK'S

This classic Simpson Bay seafood restaurant has repeatedly been voted the best on the island. Reserve a table on the water for great views of the megayachts at Isle de Sol Marina. SkipJack's sells spiny Caribbean lobster: many claim it's more flavorful than New England cold-water lobster.

Vesna Taverna

BACCHUS
With a wine cellar that puts many in mainland France to shame, Bacchus offers a stunning array of fresh French breads, pastries, and deli items. It's located in the Hope Estate area in Grand Case.

L'ASTROLABE
L'Astrolabe gets raves for its modern interpretations of classic French cuisine served around the pool at this relaxed restaurant in the Esmeralda Resort.

BIG FISH
Big portions of fresh-caught fish, sushi, and steaks are served in a modern, Miami Beach atmosphere. Try the signature spicy Hurricane Shrimp.

Best Luxury Shops in St. Barth

KALINAS PERLES

Tahitian black pearls and rare fiery pink conch pearls are among the unique finds at this shop, in addition to one-of-a-kind shells and precious stones. *Rue du Général De Gaulle, Gustavia.*

KOKON

Peruse a beautifully edited mix of designs, including accessories, shoes, and beach footwear plus designer items from the likes of Birger et Mikkelsen, Mathilde à la Plage, Clovis, bless you by Meli, and others. And shoes? Mais oui, from Heidi Klum. *Rue Fahlberg, at the head of Gustavia harbor.*

ILÉNA

A shop of gorgeous things for gorgeous people, Iléna has incredible beachwear and lingerie by Chantal Thomas, Andres Sarda, Raffaela D'Angelo, including Swarovski crystal-encrusted bikinis and seashell-encrusted bathing suits. *Villa Creole, St. Jean.*

HERMÈS

The Hermès family's creation of leather and textiles began almost 200 years ago. Hermès in St. Barth today is an independently owned franchise of the legendary business, selling leathers, silk, fragrances, footwear, clothing, and accessories. Prices are slightly less than in the U.S. *Le Carré d'Or, Gustavia.*

MADEMOISELLE HORTENSE

Charming tops and dresses are fashioned out of prints made on the island. The clothing, jewelry, bathing attire, accessories, and exquisite leather goods fills the store with a spectrum of colors. *Rue de la République, Gustavia.*

FRENCH INDIES DESIGN

This home furnishing shop on the far side of Gustavia Harbor is the brainchild of Karine Bruneel, a St. Barth-based architect and interior designer. There are lovely items to accent your home, yacht, or restaurant, including furniture, textiles, glassware, and unusual baskets, candles, and pottery. *Rive Gauche, Brigantin mansion, Gustavia.*

Kalinas Perles

FILLES DES ILES
In addition to high-quality, flattering French attire and sophisticated swimwear for all ages, this shop stocks delicious artisanal fragrances and chic accessories, like beautiful sandals.

TIME
This store specializes in exclusive watches by Breitling, Bell and Ross, Giuliano Mazzuoli, BRM, Boucheron, and more.

L.JOY BOUTIQUE
Look for lovely high-end silk tunics, evening wear, and elegant accessories.

Brides-to-be and the sparkle-obsessed can find beaded and rhinestone-set headbands and sandals.

LINEN
This shop offers tailored linen shirts for men in a rainbow of soft colors and slip-on driving mocs in classic styles.

How to Decide Between St. Maarten and St. Martin

The Caribbean is full of bucket-list destinations, which makes trying to narrow your next trip down to just one feel impossible. Luckily, St. Martin and St. Maarten allow you to hit two birds with one island. The small 37-square-mile island is split in two. Legend has it that long ago, a Frenchman and Dutchmen raced along the coast in opposite directions. When they met, the governments of France and the Netherlands split the island on that line down the middle. Today, that means visitors get treated to a unique experience: two nationalities, two different vibes—one unbeatable vacation.

Although the gateless border makes it easy to cross from one side to the other, you'll ultimately have to choose where you want to stay: the quieter, culinarily captivating French St. Martin, or the bustling Dutch St. Maarten. Let's be clear, the island is fantastic. You can't make a wrong choice when picking which side to stay on—but you can pick the side that's better for you.

FOR NATURAL BEACHES: ST. MARTIN

There's no shortage of luxuriously catered beaches across the island. You have your pick of sandy shores where you can plop down in an umbrella-shaded lounge chair and have a Caribe in your hand in five minutes. But if you're looking for something a little more secluded, a little more off the beaten track, start your search on the French side. There, you'll find hidden beaches like Happy Bay. Fifteen minutes of walking along a narrow, slightly hilly path (avoiding an occasional cow pie or two) and you'll find yourself in a gorgeous half-moon bay, with just a few other families or seminude sunbathers sharing the palm trees' shade.

INSIDER TIP: Pack a lunch or be prepared to make the short trek back to the beach bars at Friar's Bay for a midday snack—there aren't any facilities at Happy.

FOR WORLD-CLASS SHOPPING: ST. MAARTEN

On an island renowned for its (duty-free) jewelry shopping, Philipsburg's Front Street really shines above the rest. The Dutch capital is home to a number of high-class jewelry stores, as well as a charming boardwalk. When cruises are in port, the shopping areas can get crowded—all the more reason to lodge somewhere close by and pop in at your convenience!

INSIDER TIP: For more eclectic boutique-style jewelry, check out Marigot's semiweekly morning markets on the French side.

FOR FOODIES: ST. MARTIN

There's an adage that repeat visitors to the Dutch side use to sum up their decision: Stay on the Dutch side; eat on the French. That's all well and good, but why stay farther from the food than you need to? Stay on the French side and have beach-picnic brunches of fresh-baked baguettes and cheese, afternoon treats of Parisian-quality tarts, and the most sumptuous French Caribbean seafood for dinner. Book a room in Grand Case, the island's culinary capital, make reservations one night at Spiga, and then wander into one of the tiny Creole eateries called lolos the next.

FOR NUDE BEACHES: ST. MARTIN

Is there anything more French than nude sunbathing? Okay, perhaps cheese, wine, and sex appeal. But part of that last one comes from the suave self-confidence that seems innate to the French— and what could be more self-confident than baring it all? Many beaches on the French side of the island welcome nude sunbathers; some, like the ever-popular Baie Orientale, offer great happy hours if you need an extra shot of confidence to join them.

FOR BOATING CULTURE: ST. MAARTEN

The annual Heineken Regatta in the Port de Plaisance and Simpson Bay area brings crews of enthusiastic amateurs, charters, and serious sailors alike to the largest warm-water regatta in the world. It's hard to tell what the bigger draw is: the races or revelry that follows, with DJs spinning into the early hours of morning for locals and the thousands of visitors that arrive on the island each March. Any other time of the year, Simpson Bay is still a sailor's delight.

INSIDER TIP: Some of us have the means to enjoy a day—or even an entire vacation—on a yacht. For the rest of us, there are plenty of Simpson Bay bars that open up onto the marina. Gaze on the nautical opulence while sipping a (much more affordable) cocktail.

FOR THE BEST DIVING: ST. MAARTEN

There are plenty of chances to go scuba diving off the Friendly Island's shores. And while it's hard to have a bad dive in the Caribbean, the sites in St. Martin or St. Maarten don't hold a candle to some of the region's best dive spots. Nearby Saba, on the other hand! The dormant volcanic island, visible from St. Maarten's Sunset Beach on clear days, offers some of the best hidden gems for diving in the Caribbean. Ferries leave almost daily for Saba from Philipsburg or Simpson Bay, but the incomparably shorter and less nauseating flights departing from Princess Juliana International Airport are probably a better bet—even if the landing's a bit nerve-wracking!

FOR BOHO-CHIC CULTURE: ST. MARTIN

The Dutch side's almost overdeveloped infrastructure is admittedly convenient, but it also leaves some travelers feeling like that's all there is, right up until you get to the beach's edge. St. Martin's vibe, on the other hand, is half-boho, half-chic southern France. Think villas nestled into shady hills, colorful little rues in Marigot, and cafés with pastries so good you'll eat them even on a vacation where you spend 80 percent of your day in a swimsuit. On Tuesdays, check out Harmony Night in Grand Case, a festival that's equal parts open-air market and street party, with drink vendors, silversmith artisans, and crêpe-makers selling their wares as a Carnival-esque parade dances past.

FOR THE BEST TIME: ST. MARTIN/ST. MAARTEN

Whatever you do, don't stress about where you stay. American visitors might feel slightly more at home on the Dutch side, where the dollar is the default currency and English is the lingua franca, but you'll find that many vendors on the French half also speak English and will offer you a competitive dollar-to-euro exchange rate. And commitment-phobes need not worry: Crossing from one side to the other is just a matter of minutes, depending on where you are. Sleep at the little beachfront hotel nestled into the cove at Anse Marcel, then hop in your rental car for a day trip to Sunset Beach to marvel at the airport's infamously low landings. No matter which side you choose, you're making a good choice.

Family Travel

All three islands have plenty of activities and attractions that will keep children of all ages (and their parents) busy and interested. Children are generally welcome at restaurants, especially earlier in the evenings.

ST. MAARTEN/ ST. MARTIN

Le Petit Hotel, a boutique property in Grand Case, has full apartment units and a caring management team. Don't miss the ziplines at Loterie Farm or Rainforest Adventures, try kiteboarding on Orient Beach, and enjoy incredible water sports all over the island. Dig into seafood at Skipjack's, try the jerk chicken and salads at Blue Bitch Bar in Philipsburg, or grab a vegetarian bite at Top Carrot.

ST. BARTH

Children are welcome at most resorts. For a beach day, try Anse de Grand Cul de Sac for calmer, shallow waters and some bird- or turtle-watching, or pick Anse de Lorient for bigger waves. Carib Waterplay will get the young ones started with lessons for windsurfing and other activities. You can turn your beach day into a picnic with fresh to-go meals from Eden to Go.

While you're doing your own high-end shopping, you can also outfit the kids at KIWI St. Tropez or Mademoiselle Hortense. For a reasonably priced, family friendly meal out, try Les Bananier or Le Repaire Brasserie.

ANGUILLA

Aurora Resort & Spa offers children's programs, babysitting, and a great beach. Many activities are included at Cap Juluca, and Four Seasons has programs for little kids and a media room and club for teens.

Shoal Bay has shallow, gentle waters for family swimming and snorkeling, and even non-swimmers can enjoy an excursion on Junior's Glass Bottom Boat. After your day at the beach, grab some reasonably priced beach fare from Blanchards Beach Shack or tacos from Picante.

Chapter 2

TRAVEL SMART

Updated by
Riselle Celestina and
Sheryl Nance-Nash

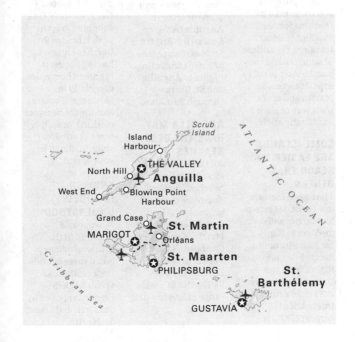

Know Before You Go

Which island is best for me? Can I get by with English? When should I go? You may have a few questions before your vacation to the Caribbean islands of St. Maarten/St. Martin, St. Barth, and Anguilla. Here's what you need to know before you embark to this tropical paradise so your next sunny holiday runs smoothly.

YOU'LL PROBABLY GO THROUGH ST. MAARTEN FIRST

These islands are close in proximity and connected by frequent ferries and flights. Most travelers, regardless of which island they plan to visit, land in St. Maarten/St. Martin and make their way to their final destination.

SOME ISLANDS ARE EASIER TO REACH THAN OTHERS

The hassle factor is low for St. Maarten/ St. Martin, and medium to high for Anguilla or St. Barth. Most nonstop flights from the United States arrive at Princess Juliana International Airport (SXM) in St. Maarten. Some American Airlines flights are direct to Anguilla from Miami. Otherwise you can get a small plane or ferry to Anguilla (AXA) or St. Barth (SBH) from St. Maarten; there are also connecting flights to Anguilla and St. Barth through San Juan.

ANGUILLA MAY HAVE THE BEST BEACHES

All three islands have beautiful beaches, but those on Anguilla are probably the best. Baie Orientale on St. Martin is one of the Caribbean's most beautiful beaches, but it's very busy. St. Barth has a wide range of lovely small beaches.

ST. MAARTEN/ST. MARTIN IS THE "FOODIE" ISLAND

While each island has amazing restaurants, St. Maarten and St. Martin stand out. The island has the most restaurants to choose from, and Grand Case in St. Martin, in particular, is renowned for being home to "restaurant row." St. Barth also attracts chefs from around the world.

ST. BARTH IS THE BEST FOR SHOPPING

Yes, St. Maarten has great duty-free shopping, but the posh island of St. Barth is known for having the most high-end boutiques, especially in Gustavia. If you're looking for designer clothing, or simply want to window-shop, St. Barth is your island.

ENGLISH IS WIDELY UNDERSTOOD

Most people involved in the tourism industry on all three islands understand and speak English; French is spoken in St. Barth and French St. Martin.

DON'T JUST VACATION IN "HIGH SEASON"

A Caribbean vacation is a great way to escape winter in much of the United States, but this is also "high season"—December 15 through April 15, especially the year-end holiday weeks. But wait! Caribbean weather doesn't change much from month to month, although late summer and early fall are generally more humid. "Low season," which is really most of the year, can be quiet, but with lower prices for accommodations and flights. The only caveat: hurricanes are at their peak in September and October.

YOU CAN USE U.S. DOLLARS

U.S. currency is accepted almost everywhere in the islands, although the standard currency in French St. Martin and St. Barth is the euro.

CORAL REEF–SAFE SUNSCREEN IS A MUST

Coral reefs are dying at an alarming rate, and one of the major contributors is sunscreen, more specifically the chemicals oxybenzone and octinoxate. Luckily, numerous companies like Sun Bum, Blue Lizard, and Thinksport offer reef-safe alternatives. So check those labels before you buy your next bottle.

THE DRINKING AGE IS DIFFERENT THAN IN THE UNITED STATES

Visitors don't have to wait until 21 to drink on these islands. Be aware of the minimum legal drinking ages, especially if you're traveling with teens: 18 in St. Maarten/St. Martin and St. Barth, 16 in Anguilla.

AMERICANS NEED A PASSPORT

A valid passport is required to enter or reenter the United States from these islands. U.S. tourists do not need a visa to travel here.

SHOULD YOU TIP?

Most restaurants add a service charge of 15%. It's not necessary to tip once a service charge has been added to the bill, but sometimes that tip is shared among all staff. If the service is good, an additional tip of 10% is always appreciated. If no service charge is included on the final bill, then leave the customary tip of 15% to 20%.

ACCOMMODATIONS VARY BY ISLAND

St. Maarten has several large resorts, a range of smaller hotels and villas, and many time-shares available for rent in the off-season. On St. Martin smaller hotels predominate, though there are also some large resorts and private villas. On St. Barth, most visitors stay in villas or small hotels. Anguilla has some large resorts, as well as smaller hotels and villas.

Getting Here and Around

St. Maarten/St. Martin, St. Barthélemy, and Anguilla are part of a cluster of islands in the Lesser Antilles that are fairly close together. In fact, the islands are linked by both frequent ferries and small-plane flights. St. Maarten/St. Martin, which has the only international airport among the three capable of handling large passenger jets, is the international flight hub. Most travelers, regardless of which island they plan to visit, land in St. Maarten/St. Martin and make their way to their final destination.

 Air

ST. MAARTEN/ ST. MARTIN

More than 20 carriers fly to the island. There are nonstop flights from Atlanta (Delta, seasonal), Boston (JetBlue, seasonal), Charlotte (American), Miami/Ft. Lauderdale (American and JetBlue), New York–JFK (American, Delta, JetBlue), Newark, Chicago, and Dulles (United, seasonal), Ft. Lauderdale (JetBlue, Spirit), Orlando (Frontier), and Philadelphia (American). Nonstop flights also arrive from both Paris (Air France) and Amsterdam (KLM) as well as Panama (Copa, which has many connections

from and to the United States). There are also direct flights from Montreal and Toronto and some nonstop charter flights (including some from Boston). You can also connect in San Juan on Seabourne and Winair, the St. Maarten–based local carrier. Many smaller Caribbean-based airlines, including Air Caraïbes, Air Antilles, Anguilla Air Services, Caribbean Airlines, Air Sunshine, St. Barth Commuter, and Winair (Windward Islands Airways), offer service from other islands in the Caribbean.

ST. BARTHÉLEMY

Because of its tiny, hillside runway, there are no direct major-airline flights to St. Barth. Most North Americans fly first into St. Maarten's Princess Juliana International SXM Airport, from which the island is a quick 15 minutes by air. Winair has frequent flights from St. Maarten every day. Through Winair's affiliation with major airlines, you can check your luggage from your home airport through to St. Barth under certain circumstances. Tradewind Aviation has regularly scheduled service from San Juan and also does VIP charters. Anguilla Air Services and St. Barth Commuter have scheduled flights and also do charters. *Leave ample time between your scheduled flight and your*

connection in St. Maarten:
90 minutes is the minimum
recommended (and be aware
that luggage frequently doesn't
make the trip; your hotel or villa-rental company may be able
to send someone to retrieve
it). It's a good idea to pack a
change of clothes, required
medicines, and a bathing suit
in your carry-on—or better yet,
pack very light and don't check
baggage at all.

ANGUILLA

American Airlines' inaugural
flight from Miami to Anguilla in
2021 marked the beginning of
nonstop flights to Anguilla from
the United States. American
has two to three flights per
week from Miami, depending
on the time of year. You can
also get here fast by flying to
St. Maarten's Princess Juliana
International SXM Airport and
taking a nearby ferry to Anguilla, about a half-hour ride away.
Air Sunshine also flies several
times a day from St. Thomas
and San Juan, Cape Air from
St. Thomas once a week, and
Anguilla Air Services flies from
St. Maarten and St. Barth.
Silver Airway flies in from San
Juan. TransAnguilla provides
scheduled flights throughout
the Caribbean.

Boat

ST. MAARTEN/ ST. MARTIN

You can take ferries to St. Barth
(45–60 minutes, €55–€90 from
the French side, though you
can pay in dollars or $85–$115
from the Dutch side); to Anguilla (25 minutes, €25 from the
French side); and to Saba (one
to two hours, $90–$100 from
the Dutch side).

ST. BARTHÉLEMY

St. Barth can be reached
via ferry service from St.
Maarten/St. Martin to Quai
de la République in Gustavia.
Voyager offers at least twice
daily round-trips for about
$100, economy class per per-
son from Marigot. Great Bay
Express has multiple round-
trips daily from the Dutch side
of Sint Maarten for roughly
€110 if reserved in advance,
€115 for same-day tickets, and
€70 each way for a same-day
round-trip. Private boat charters are also available, but they
are very expensive; MasterSki
Pilou offers transfers from St.
Maarten.

ANGUILLA

Public ferries run frequently
between Anguilla and Marigot
on French St. Martin. Boats
leave from Blowing Point on
Anguilla three times daily
(same from Marigot,

Getting Here and Around

St. Martin) between 7 am and 6 pm. You pay a $23 departure tax before boarding ($5 for day-trippers coming through the Blowing Point terminal—but be sure to make this clear at the window where you pay), in addition to the $20 one-way fare. Fares require cash payment. Children under 12 years of age are $10. On very windy days the 20-minute trip can be fairly bouncy. The drive between the Marigot ferry terminal and the St. Maarten airport is vastly faster thanks to the causeway (bridge) across Simpson Bay lagoon. Transfers by speedboat to Anguilla are available from a terminal right at the airport at a cost of about $85 per person (arranged directly with a company or through your Anguilla hotel). Private ferry companies listed below run four or more round-trips a day, coinciding with major flights, between Blowing Point and Princess Juliana airport in Dutch St. Maarten. On the St. Maarten side they will bring you right to the terminal in a van, or you can just walk across the parking lot. These trips are $75 one-way or $130 round-trip (cash only) and usually include departure taxes. There are also private charters available.

 ## Car

ST. MAARTEN/ ST. MARTIN

It's easy to get around the island by car. Virtually all roads are paved and in generally good condition. However, they can be crowded, especially during high season; you might experience traffic jams, particularly around Marigot around noon and Simpson Bay from 3 pm. Be alert for occasional potholes and unpainted speed bumps (small signs warn you), as well as the island tradition of stopping in the middle of the road to chat with a friend or yield to someone entering traffic. Be aware that there is no stopping in a roundabout to allow someone to enter the roundabout. Few roads are identified by name or number, but most have signs indicating the destination. Driving is on the right. There are gas stations all over the island, but gas tends to be cheaper on the French side.

Car Rentals: You can book a car at Princess Juliana International SXM Airport, where all major rental companies have booths, but it is often *much* cheaper to reserve a car in advance from home. That's also an especially wise move in high season when some companies may run out of cars. A shuttle to the rental-car companies' lots is provided. Rates are among the best in the Caribbean, as little as $25–$40 per day in low season, but at least $240/week, and up, in high season. You can also rent a car on the French side, but this rarely makes sense for Americans because of the exchange rates.

ST. BARTHÉLEMY

Roads are sometimes unmarked, so get a map and look for signs, nailed to posts at all crossroads, pointing to a destination. Roads are narrow and sometimes very steep, but have been improved; even so, check the brakes and low gears before driving away from the rental office. Maximum speed is 30 mph (50 kph). Driving is on the right, as in the United States and Europe. Parking is an additional challenge. There are two gas stations on the island, one near the airport and one in Lorient. They aren't open after 5 pm or on Sunday, and pumps at the station near the airport now accept chip-and-pin credit cards. Considering the short distances, a full tank should last most of a week.

■ TIP→ Ask your car rental company about Blue Parking Tags, which give you 1½ hours of parking for free.

Car Rentals: You must have a valid driver's license and be 25 or older to rent, and in high

season there may be a three-day minimum. During peak periods, such as Christmas week and February, arrange for your car rental ahead of time. Rental agencies operate out of Jean Remi de Haenen airport; some will bring your car to your hotel. Alternately, when you make your hotel reservation, ask if the hotel has its own cars available to rent; some hotels provide 24-hour emergency road service—something most rental companies don't. Expect to pay at least $55 per day, and note the company will usually hold about $500 until the car is returned.

■ TIP→ For a green alternative, consider renting an electric car. They're available for about $85 per day.

ANGUILLA

Although many of the rental cars on-island have the driver's side on the left as in North America, Anguillian roads are like those in the United Kingdom—driving is on the left side of the road. It's easy to get the hang of, but the roads can be rough, so be cautious, and observe the 30 mph (48 kph) speed limit. Roundabouts are probably the biggest driving obstacle for most. As you approach, give way to the vehicle on your right; once you're in the roundabout, you have the right of way.

Getting Here and Around

Car Rentals: A temporary Anguilla driver's license is required to rent a car—you can get into real trouble if you're caught driving without one. You get it for $20 (good for three months) through any of the car-rental agencies at the time you pick up your car; you'll also need your valid driver's license from home. Rental rates start at about $45 to $55 per day, plus insurance.

🚲 Moped, Scooter, and Bike

ST. BARTHÉLEMY

Several companies rent motorbikes, scooters, mopeds, ATVs, and mountain bikes. Motorbikes go for about $30 per day and require a $100 deposit. ATV rental starts at $40 per day. Helmets are required. Scooter and motorbike rental places are mostly along rue de France in Gustavia and around the airport in St-Jean. If you have not driven an ATV or "quad" before, St. Barth may not be the best place to try it out. The roads, though not jammed with traffic, are quite narrow, and navigating the hilly terrain can be quite a challenge.

Taxi

ST. MAARTEN/ ST. MARTIN

There is a government-sponsored taxi dispatcher at the airport and the harbor. Posted fares are for one or two people. Add $5 for each additional person, half price for kids. The first bag is free; after that it's $1 per bag. It costs about $18 from the airport to Philipsburg or Marigot, and about $30 to Dawn Beach. After 10 pm fares go up 25%, and after midnight 50%. Licensed drivers can be identified by the "taxi" or new "T" license plate on the Dutch side and the TXI license plate on the French side. Avoid any uninsured illegal cabs that may appear; they have no such plates, and police have been cracking down on them across the island. Fixed fares apply from Juliana International Airport and the Marigot ferry to hotels around the island.

ST. BARTHÉLEMY

Taxis are expensive and not particularly easy to arrange, especially in the evening. There's a taxi station at the airport and another at the ferry dock in Gustavia; from elsewhere you must contact a dispatcher in Gustavia or St-Jean. Fares are regulated by the Collectivity, and drivers accept both dollars and euros. If you go out to dinner by taxi, let the restaurant know if you will need a taxi at the end of the meal, and they will call one for you.

ANGUILLA

Taxis are fairly expensive, so if you plan to explore many beaches and restaurants, it may be more cost-effective to rent a car. Taxi rates are regulated by the government, and there are fixed fares from point to point, listed in brochures the drivers should have handy and published in local guides. It's about $22 from the airport or $28 from Blowing Point Ferry to West End hotels. Posted rates are for one or two people; each additional passenger adds $5, and there is a $1 charge for each piece of luggage beyond the allotted two. You can also hire a taxi for a flat rate of $28 an hour. A surcharge of $4 applies to trips between 6 pm and midnight. After midnight it's $10. You'll always find taxis at the Blowing Point Ferry landing and the airport at the taxi dispatch, but you'll need to call for hotel and restaurant pickups and arrange ahead with the driver who took you if you need a late-night return from a nightclub or bar.

Essentials

🍴 Dining

St. Maarten/St. Martin, Anguilla, and St. Barth are known for their fine restaurants.

For more information on local cuisine and dining possibilities, see the individual island chapters.

For information on food-related health issues, see Health below.

PAYING

Credit cards are widely accepted on all three islands.

For more information, see the individual island chapters.

📍 Electricity

Generally, Dutch St. Maarten and Anguilla operate on 110 volts AC (60-cycle) and have outlets that accept flat-prong plugs—the same as in North America. You will need neither an adaptor nor a transformer on these islands.

French St. Martin and St. Barth operate on 220 volts AC (60-cycle), with round-prong plugs, as in Europe; you'll need an adapter and sometimes a converter for North American appliances. The French outlets have a safety mechanism—equal pressure must be applied to both prongs of the plug to connect to the socket. Most hotels have hair dryers, so you should not need to bring one (but ask your hotel to be sure), and some hotels have shaver outlets in the bathroom that accept North American electrical plugs.

➕ Health

There's been a sharp decrease in cases of mosquito-borne illnesses including Dengue Fever, Chikungunya, and Zika across the region thanks to increased vigilance by all three islands' governments in the wake of cases reported in the mid '00s. Still, you should be cautious. Although there are no effective vaccines to prevent them, visitors to the region should protect themselves with mosquito repellent (particularly repellent containing DEET, which has been deemed the most effective) and keep arms and legs covered at sunset, when some mosquitoes may be particularly active.

COVID-19 has disrupted travel since March 2020, and travelers should expect sporadic ongoing issues. Always travel with a mask in case it's required, and keep up to date on the most recent testing and vaccination guidelines for whatever island you're traveling to.

There are no particular ongoing problems regarding food and water safety in St. Maarten/St. Martin, Anguilla, or St. Barth. If you have an especially sensitive stomach, you may wish to drink only bottled water; also be sure that food has been thoroughly cooked and is served to you fresh and hot. Peel fruit. If you have problems, mild cases of traveler's diarrhea may respond to Pepto-Bismol. Imodium may be necessary if you have persistent problems. Be sure to drink plenty of fluids; if you can't keep fluids down, seek medical help immediately.

MEDICAL INSURANCE AND ASSISTANCE

Consider buying trip insurance with medical-only coverage. Neither Medicare nor some private insurers cover medical expenses anywhere outside the United States. Medical-only policies typically reimburse you for medical care (excluding that related to pre-existing conditions) and hospitalization abroad. Consider programs like "SkyMed," which takes Americans and Canadians back to their home-city hospitals instead of "to the nearest appropriate facility," which is what most credit-card based medical evacuation insurance plans actually do.

Immunizations

No specific immunizations or vaccinations are required for visits to the Caribbean islands, but children should be up-to-date on their routine immunizations (DTaP, MMR, influenza, chicken pox, and polio). Travellers who are not fully vaccinated for COVID-19 may be subject to testing and other requirements; check with your destination for current guidelines and plan on getting tested within 48 hours before your arrival.

Lodging

ST. MAARTEN/ ST. MARTIN

St. Maarten/St. Martin has the widest array of accommodations of any of the three islands, with a range of large resort hotels, small resorts, time-shares, condos, private villas, and small bed-and-breakfasts scattered across the island. Most of the larger resorts are concentrated in Dutch St. Maarten. Visitors find a wide range of choices in many different price ranges.

ST. BARTHÉLEMY

The vast majority of accommodations on St. Barth are in private villas in a wide variety of levels of luxury and price;

Essentials

villas are often priced in U.S. dollars. The island's small luxury hotels are exceedingly expensive, made more so for Americans because prices are in euros. A few modest and moderately priced hotels do exist on the island, but there's nothing on St. Barth that could be described as cheap, though there are now a few simple guesthouses and inns that offer acceptable accommodations for what in St. Barth is a bargain price (not far over €100 per night in low season in some cases).

ANGUILLA

Anguilla has several large luxury resorts, a few smaller resorts and guesthouses, and a rather large mix of private condos and villas. Lodging on Anguilla is generally fairly expensive, but there are a few more modestly priced choices.

$ Money

Prices throughout this guide are given for adults. Substantially reduced fees are almost always available for children, students, and senior citizens. Refrences to credit cards are made only in those cases where they are not accepted.

ST. MAARTEN/ ST. MARTIN

Legal tender on the Dutch side is the Netherlands Antilles florin (guilder) but almost everyone accepts U.S. dollars. On the French side, the currency is the euro, but most establishments accept dollars. At this writing, quite a few restaurants continue to offer one-to-one euro-for-dollar equivalency for purchases made in cash. ATMs dispense dollars, euros, or guilders, depending on where you are.

ST. BARTHÉLEMY

Legal tender is the euro, but U.S. dollars are widely accepted. ATMs are common and dispense only euros.

ANGUILLA

Legal tender is the Eastern Caribbean (EC) dollar, but U.S. dollars are widely accepted. ATMs dispense both U.S. and EC dollars.

All prices quoted in this chapter are in U.S. dollars.

🌐 Passport

A valid passport and a return or ongoing ticket is required for travel to Anguilla, St. Barthélemy, and St. Maarten/St. Martin. There are no border controls whatsoever between the Dutch and French sides of St.

Maarten/St. Martin. Passports must be valid for at least three months from the date of entry to the territory of St. Barthélemy.

Visa

Visas are not required for travelers with a passport issued by the United States to a Caribbean nation. Passport-holders from the Middle East, African nations, most of Asia, and parts of Central and South America must apply for a tourist visa.

➕ Safety

ST. MAARTEN/ ST. MARTIN

Though the island fairly safe, theft and street crime does occur on both sides. Additionally, the island is sometimes used by drug smugglers; while this typically does not affect tourists, you should be careful not to leave bags unattended, and do not agree to carry packages for others. Always lock your valuables and travel documents in your room safe or your hotel's front-desk safe; carry only your drivers license or a photocopy of your passport with you for identification. Don't leave anything in the car,

even in the trunk or glove compartment. When driving, keep your seatbelt on and the car doors locked. Don't drink and drive; penalties for violating the law are severe. Never leave anything unattended at the beach. Despite the romantic imagery of the Caribbean, it's not good policy to take long walks along the beach at night, and you should be aware of your surroundings even during the day. Carry your handbag securely and zipped, don't flash cash or jewelry, and park in the busier and better-lit areas of parking lots.

ST. BARTHÉLEMY

There's relatively little crime on St. Barth, though you should take basic precautions. Most hotel rooms have safes for your valuables and personal documents; don't tempt loss by leaving cameras, laptops, or jewelry out in plain sight in your hotel room or villa or in your car. Don't walk barefoot at night: there are venomous centipedes that can inflict a remarkably painful sting. If you ask residents, they will tell you that they only drink bottled water, although most cook or make coffee with tap water.

ANGUILLA

Anguilla is a quiet, relatively safe island, but robberies and other crimes do occur. Don't tempt fate by leaving your

Essentials

valuables unattended in your hotel room, on the beach, or in your car; most hotel rooms are equipped with a safe. Be wary of remote beaches, and lock your car, hotel room, and villa.

Taxes

ST. MAARTEN/ ST. MARTIN

Departure tax from Juliana Airport is $10 to destinations within the Netherlands Antilles and $30 to all other destinations—this is usually included in your air ticket. It will cost you €3 (usually included in the ticket price) to depart by plane from Aéroport de L'Espérance and $3 (the rate can change) by ferry to Anguilla from Marigot's pier. Hotels on the Dutch side add a 15% service charge to the bill as well as a 5% government tax. Hotels on the French side add a 10%–15% service charge and generally 5% tax.

ST. BARTHÉLEMY

The island charges a $5 departure tax when your next stop is another French island, $10 to anywhere else payable in cash only (dollars or euros). Some hotels add a 10% service charge. Sometimes it is included in the room rate, so check. There is a 5% room tax on hotels and villa rentals.

ANGUILLA

A departure tax of $25 for people 12 and over is payable at the airport or Blowing Point Ferry Terminal—credit cards may be accepted but it's a good idea to have cash on hand in case there's an issue. If you are staying in Anguilla but day-tripping to St. Martin, be sure to mention it, and the rate will be only $8. A 10% accommodations tax is added to hotel bills.

Time

St. Maarten, Anguilla, and St. Barth are in the Atlantic Standard Time zone, which is one hour later than Eastern Standard and four hours earlier than GMT. Caribbean islands don't observe daylight saving time, so during the period when it's in effect, Atlantic Standard and Eastern Daylight Savings Time are the same.

Tipping

ST. MAARTEN/ ST. MARTIN

Service charges may be added to hotel and restaurant bills on the Dutch side (otherwise tip 15%–18%). Check bills carefully so you don't inadvertently tip twice. On the French side, a service charge is customary; on top of the included service it is customary to leave an extra 5%–10% *in cash* for the server. Taxi drivers, porters, and maids depend on tips.

ST. BARTHÉLEMY

Restaurants include a 15% service charge in their published prices, but it's common French practice to leave 5% to 10% more in cash, even if you have paid by credit card. Most taxi drivers don't expect a tip.

ANGUILLA

Despite any service charge, it's usually expected that you will tip more—$5 per day for housekeeping, $20 for a helpful concierge, and $10 per day to beach attendants. Many restaurants include a service charge of 10% to 15% on the bill; if there's no surcharge, tip about 15%. Taxi drivers usually receive 10% of the fare.

📅 When to Go

The Caribbean high season runs from about December 15 through April 15—great for escaping winter. The Christmas holiday season is very busy in St. Martin/St. Maarten and an especially expensive time to visit Anguilla and St. Barth, and you may very well pay double during this period, with minimum rental requirements

for some villas and hotels. After April prices may be 20% to 50% less, and you can often book on short notice. Some hotels and restaurants close for all or part of September and October.

CLIMATE

The average year-round temperatures for the region are 78°F to 88°F. The temperature extremes are 65°F low, 95°F high; but, as everyone knows, it's the humidity, not the heat, that makes you suffer—especially when the two go hand in hand. The high-season months of December through April generally provide warm, sunny days with little humidity. The off-season months, particularly August through November, are the most humid. As part of the late-fall rainy season, hurricanes occasionally sweep through the Caribbean. Check the news daily and keep abreast of brewing tropical storms. The rainy season consists mostly of brief showers interspersed with sunshine. You can watch the clouds thicken, feel the rain, then have brilliant sunshine dry you off, all while remaining on your lounge chair. A spell of overcast days or heavy rainfall is unusual.

HURRICANE SEASON

The Atlantic hurricane season lasts from June 1 through November 30, but it's fairly rare

Essentials

to see a large storm in either June or November. Most major hurricanes occur between August and October, with the peak season in September. Since 2017's Hurricane Irma, hotels and restaurants have rebuilt stronger and standards have been raised to a much higher level.

If a hurricane warning is issued and flights to your destination are disrupted, virtually every Caribbean resort will waive cancellation and change penalties and allow you to rebook your trip for a later date. Some will allow you to cancel if a hurricane threatens to strike, even if flights aren't canceled. Some will give you a refund if you have prepaid for your stay, while others will expect you to rebook your trip for a later date. Some large resort companies—including Sandals and SuperClubs—have "hurricane guarantees," but they apply only when flights have been canceled or when a hurricane is sure to strike.

If you plan to travel to the Caribbean during the hurricane season, it is wise to buy travel insurance that allows you to cancel for any reason. This kind of coverage can be expensive (up to 10% of the value of the trip); but if you have to prepay far in advance for an expensive vacation package, the peace of mind may be worth it. Just be sure to read the fine print; some policies don't kick in unless flights are canceled and the hurricane strikes, something you may not be assured of until the day you plan to travel. To get a complete cancellation policy, you must usually buy your insurance within a week of booking your trip. If you wait to purchase insurance until after the hurricane warning is issued, it will be too late.

To keep a close eye on the Caribbean during hurricane season, several websites track hurricanes as they progress: ⊕ *www.accuweather.com*, ⊕ *hurricanetrack.com*, ⊕ *www.nhc.noaa.gov*, and ⊕ *www.weather.com*.

Weddings and Honeymoons

There's no question that St. Maarten/St. Martin, St. Barth, and Anguilla are three of the Caribbean's foremost honeymoon destinations. Romance is in the air here, and the white, sandy beaches and turquoise water, swaying palm trees, balmy tropical breezes, and perpetual summer sunshine put people in the mood for love. Destination weddings—no longer exclusive to celebrities and the super rich—are also popular on Anguilla and Dutch St. Maarten, but French residency requirements make getting married in French St. Martin or St. Barth too difficult. All the larger resorts in Anguilla and St. Maarten have wedding planners to help you with the paperwork and details.

THE BIG DAY
Choosing the Perfect Place.
When choosing a location, remember that you really have two choices to make: the ceremony location and where to have the reception, if you're having one. For the former, there are beaches, bluffs overlooking beaches, gardens, private residences, resort lawns, and, of course, places of worship. As for the reception, there are these same choices, as well as restaurants. If you decide to go outdoors, remember the seasons (yes, the Caribbean has seasons). Be sure you have a backup plan

in case it rains. If your heart is set on an outdoor wedding at sunset, match the time of your ceremony to the time the sun sets at that time of year.

Finding a Wedding Planner. If you're planning to invite more than an officiant and your loved one to your wedding ceremony, seriously consider on-island wedding planners who can help with selecting a location, designing the floral decor, and recommending a reliable photographer. They can plan the menu, and suggest local traditions to incorporate into your ceremony. Of course, all the larger resorts have their own wedding planners. If you're planning a resort wedding, work with the on-site wedding coordinator to prepare a detailed list of the exact services they'll provide. If your idea of your wedding doesn't match their services, try a different resort. Or look for an independent wedding planner. Both Anguilla and St. Maarten have independent wedding planners who are not employed by resorts.

Legal Requirements. There are minimal residency requirements on Anguilla and St. Maarten, and no blood tests or shots are required on either island. On Anguilla, you can get a wedding license in two working days; paperwork in St.

Weddings and Honeymoons

Maarten has to be submitted 14 days in advance, but there is no residency requirement there. You need to supply proof of identity (a passport or certified copy of your birth certificate signed by a notary public, though in Anguilla even a driver's license with a photo will do). You must provide proof of divorce with the original or certified copy of the divorce decree if you are divorced, or copy of the death certificate if you are a widow or widower.

Wedding Attire. In the Caribbean, basically anything goes, from long, formal dresses with trains to white bikinis. Floral sundresses are fine, too. Men can wear tuxedos or a simple pair of solid-color slacks with a nice white linen shirt. If you want formal dress and a tuxedo, it's usually better to bring your formal attire with you.

Photographs. Deciding whether to use the photographer supplied by your resort or an independent photographer is an important choice. Resorts that host a lot of weddings usually have their own photographers, but you can also find independent, professional island-based photographers, and an independent wedding planner will know the best in the area. Look at the portfolio (many photographers now have websites), and decide whether this person can give you the kind of memories you are looking for. If you're satisfied with the photographer that your resort uses, then make sure you see proofs and order prints before you leave the island. In any case, arrange to take a CD home with you of HD photos, because uploading them via the Internet is a time-consuming frustration what with (typically slow) Caribbean connections.

THE HONEYMOON

Do you want champagne and strawberries delivered to your room each morning? An infinity pool in which to float? A five-star restaurant in which to dine? Then a resort is the way to go, and both Anguilla and St. Maarten have options in different price ranges (though Anguilla resorts are more luxurious and more expensive as a rule). Whether you want a luxurious experience or a more modest one, you'll certainly find someplace romantic to which you can escape. You can usually stay on at the resort where your wedding was held. On the other hand, maybe you want your own private home. In that case, a private vacation-rental home or condo is the answer.

On the Calendar

January

St. Barth Music Festival.
Showcasing a wide variety of musical and dance performances, the festival is usually held the second and third weeks of the month. ⊕ *www.stbartsmusicfestival.org*

February

St. Barth Carnival. In St. Barth, celebrations take place in February and early March, ending with a bang on Fat Tuesday.

March

Moonsplash, Anguilla. Visiting musicians join regional reggae superstar Bankie Banx for this annual music festival.

St. Maarten Heineken Regatta. The regatta in early March brings sailors and partygoers from all over the world. As many as 300 sailboats from around the world compete. ⊕ *heinekenregatta.com*

SXM Music Festival. This five-day music festival in St. Martin features a lineup of electronic and house musicians. ⊕ *www.sxmfestival.com*

April

Festival del Mar, Anguilla. Celebrate Anguilla culture during this Easter weekend festival at Island Harbour.

Les Voiles de Saint Barth. An international regatta draws crowds.

St. Maarten Carnival. The big event follows Easter with parades, great food, and music for all.

May

Anguilla Day. Mark your calendar for May 30, when there is a round-the-island race.

Anguilla Regatta. The national love for boat racing peaks at this event.

St. Barth Festival of Caribbean Cinema. Celebrate Caribbean-made documentaries and feature films. ⊕ *www.stbarthff.org*

July

Bastille Day. St. Barth and St. Martin both celebrate this French holiday of the storming of the Bastille, which kicked off the French Revolution, with fireworks.

On the Calendar

August

Anguilla Summer Festival. Starting the first Monday in August, the races of old-fashioned wooden boats are accompanied by 10 days of nonstop partying. The "landracers" following onshore have as much fun as the boats.

November

Culinary Month, St. Maarten. A month of events makes this foodie destination paradise.

St. Barth Gourmet Festival. A celebration of French cuisine featuring prestigious guest chefs. ⊕ *saintbarthgourmet-festival.com/en/us/*

December

New Year's Eve, St. Barth. Locals join visiting boats for a round-the-island regatta, and a fantastic fireworks display over Gustavia Harbor.

Great Itineraries

Here are some suggestions for how to make the most of your trip to the islands, whichever one you choose.

A PERFECT DAY IN ST. MAARTEN/ST. MARTIN

On the French side (St. Martin)? In the morning head to Loterie Farm on the slopes of Pic Paradis to take advantage of the hiking trails or try the zipline, a favorite activity for families. You can stay and have lunch in the café, and lounge around the beautiful spring-fed swimming pool. If you are hot, head right to Baie Orientale, where you can rent some chairs and umbrellas from one of the beach clubs and take advantage of the lovely surf. If you get hungry, you can have snacks or lunch there, too. In the late afternoon, a nap is in order, but you have to be awake before sunset. For a splurge, have your sunset cocktail at the bar of Belmond La Samanna before heading to one of the restaurants in Grand Case like La Cigale for a perfect dinner.

If you're on the Dutch side, St. Maarten, try the zipline in Philipsburg for views high above the bustling town, or choose a beach for a more relaxed morning. Cupecoy and Simpson Bay are both top-notch, and Maho Beach is a top choice for watching planes fly low overhead. The afternoon is a good time to stroll along Front Street in Philipsburg, because you can duck into one of the many air-conditioned stores to escape the heat (and take advantage of duty-free shopping). For dinner, head to Izi Ristorante Italiano in Simpson Bay and cap off the night with a drink at Karakter Beach Lounge or Ocean Lounge.

A PERFECT DAY IN ST. BARTH

Have your café au lait and croissant in a harborside café in Gustavia, and explore some of the many boutiques on Quai de la République. If you tire of the hubbub, have lunch in quieter St-Jean and then shop and stroll some more. If you're not a shopper, tie on your sneakers and hike for half an hour down the path to the secluded cove at Colombier, take a snorkeling excursion, or go deep-sea fishing. Be sure to get a late-afternoon nap, because the nightlife in St. Barth doesn't get going until late. After a sunset cocktail in Gustavia, have dinner at one of the island's many great restaurants. Perhaps you'll choose Le Toiny, with its excellent views, or Le Ti St. Barth Caribbean Tavern, which is as much a gathering spot as a restaurant. By the time dessert comes, someone is sure to be dancing on the tables.

Great Itineraries

Late-night partying really gets going after midnight.

A PERFECT DAY IN ANGUILLA

The perfect day in Anguilla often involves the least activity. After breakfast, head to powdery Shoal Bay. If you get tired of sunning and dozing, take a ride on Junior's Glass Bottom Boat, or arrange a wreck dive at Shoal Bay Scuba Shack. Have lunch at one of the beachside restaurants and relax a little more. In the late afternoon, head back to your hotel room to shower and change before going to Elvis' Beach Bar to watch the sunset with a cold rum punch. Have dinner at one of the island's great restaurants.

Contacts

Air

AIRPORTS

Aéroport de L'Espérance (SFG). ✉ *Rte. de l'Espérance, Grand Case* ☎ *0590/27–11–00* ⊕ *www.saintmartin-airport. com.* **Clayton J. Lloyd International Airport.** ☎ *264/497–3510* ⊕ *www.gov.ai/airport.php.* **Jean Remi de Haenen (SBH).** ✉ *St. Jean Rd., St-Jean* ☎ *0590/27–75–81.* **Princess Juliana International Airport (SXM).** ☎ *721/546–7542* ⊕ *www. sxmairport.com.*

AIRLINE CONTACTS

Air Caraïbes. ✉ *Rte. de l'Espérance* ☎ *0590/87–10–36* ⊕ *www.aircaraibes.com.* **American Airlines.** ☎ *721/545–2040 Local SXM number for reservations, 800/433–7300 AA's main number* ⊕ *www.aa.com.* **Caribbean Airlines.** ☎ *721/546–7610* ⊕ *www.caribbean-airlines.com.* **Delta Airlines.** ☎ *721/546–7615, 800/221–1212* ⊕ *www.delta. com.* **JetBlue.** ☎ *721/546–7797, 800/538–2583* ⊕ *www. jetblue.com.* **St. Barth Commuter.** ☎ *0590/27–54–54* ⊕ *www. stbarthcommuter.com.* **United Airlines.** ☎ *800/864–8331* ⊕ *www.united.com.* **Winair.** ☎ *721/545–4237* ⊕ *www.fly-winair.sx.*

LOCAL AIRLINE CONTACTS

Anguilla Air Services. ☎ *264/498–5922* ⊕ *www. anguillaairservices.com.* **Trans Anguilla Airways.** ☎ *264/498–5922* ⊕ *www. transanguilla.com.* **St. Barth Commuter.** ☎ *0590/27–54–54* ⊕ *www.stbarthcommuter.com.* **Tradewind Aviation.** ☎ *203/267–3305* ⊕ *www.flytradewind. com.* **Winair.** ☎ *0590/27–61–01, 866/545-4237* ⊕ *www.fly-winair.com.*

Car

CAR-RENTAL CONTACTS

Avis. ✉ *Airport Rd., Simpson Bay* ☎ *888/777–2847, 721/545-2847* ⊕ *www.avis.com.* **Budget.** ☎ *800/472–3325, 721/587-2847* ⊕ *www.sxmbudget.com.* **Dollar/Thrifty Car Rental.** ✉ *102 Airport Rd.* ☎ *721/545–2393* ⊕ *www.dollarthriftysxm.com.* **Empress Rent-a-Car.** ☎ *721/545-2062* ⊕ *www.empressrentacar. com.* **Golfe Car Rental.** ✉ *Rte. de l'Espérance, Grand Case* ☎ *0690/35–04–75* ⊕ *www. golfecarrental.com.* **Hertz.** ✉ *82 Airport Rd., Simpson Bay* ☎ *721/545–4541* ⊕ *www.hertz. sxmrentacar.com.* **Unity Car Rental.** ✉ *6 Sister Modesta Rd., Simpson Bay* ☎ *721/520–5767* ⊕ *www.unitycarrental.com.* **Turbé.** ☎ *0590/27–71–42* ⊕ *www.turbe-car-rental.com.*

Contacts

Gumbs. ☎ 0590/27–75–32 ⊕ www.gumbs-car-rental.com. **Andy's Auto Rental.** ✉ Blowing Point Village ☎ 264/584–7010, 264/235-7010 Whatsapp ⊕ www.andyrentals.com. **Bryans Car Rental.** ✉ Blowing Point Village ☎ 203/992-5407 from the US, 264/497–6407 ⊕ www.bryanscarrentals.com. **Barthloc Rental.** ✉ Rue de France, Gustavia ☎ 0590/27–52–81 ⊕ www.barthloc.com. **Chez Béranger.** ✉ 21 rue du général de Gaulle, Gustavia ☎ 0590/27–89–00 ⊕ www.beranger-rental.com.

🅾 Ferry

ST. MAARTEN/ST. MARTIN FERRIES

Aqua Mania Adventures. ✉ Simpson Bay Resort Marina Plaza, Simpson Bay ☎ 721/544–2640 ⊕ www.stmaarten-activities.com. **Great Bay Express.** ✉ Bobby's Marina Village, Philipsburg ☎ 721/542–0032 Dutch side ⊕ www.greatbayexpress.com. **Link Ferries.** ✉ Marigot ☎ 264/772–4901 ⊕ www.linkferry.com. **Voyager.** ✉ Marigot ☎ 0590/87–10–68 ⊕ www.voy12.com.

ST. BARTHÉLEMY BOAT AND FERRY CONTACTS

Great Bay Express. ✉ Quai Gustavia, Gustavia ☎ 721/520–5015 ⊕ www.greatbayexpress.com. **Master Ski Pilou.** ☎ 0590/27–91–79 ⊕ www.masterski-pilou. com. **Voyager.** ☎ 0590/87–10–68 ⊕ www.voy12.com.

ANGUILLA CONTACTS

Funtime Ferry. ☎ 264/497–6511 ⊕ www.funtimecharters.com. **Link Ferries.** ☎ 264/772–4901 ⊕ www.linkferry.com.

🚕 Taxi

Juliana Airport Taxi Dispatch. ☎ 721/542–1681 ⊕ www.sxmairporttaxis.com. **Taxi Prestige.** ☎ 0590/27–70–57.

➕ Health and Safety

EMERGENCY SERVICES

Dutch-side emergencies. ☎ 911, 721/542–2222. **French-side emergencies.** ☎ 17 Police emergency, 15 Medical emergency.

📍 Visitor Information

St Maarten Tourist Information Bureau. ☎ 721/549–0200 ⊕ www.vacationstmaarten. com. **St Martin Office de Tourisme.** ✉ Rte. de Sandy Ground, Marigot ⊕ www.st-martin.org. **St Barts Office du Tourisme.** ✉ 10 rue de France, Gustavia ☎ 0590/27–87–27 ⊕ www.saintbarth-tourisme. com. **Anguilla Tourist Board.** ✉ Coronation Ave., The Valley ☎ 264/497–2759 ⊕ www.ivisitanguilla.com.

ST. MAARTEN/ ST. MARTIN

Updated by
Riselle Celestina

👁 Sights   🍴 Restaurants   🛏 Hotels   🛍 Shopping   🍸 Nightlife

★★★★★   ★★★★★   ★★★★☆   ★★★★★   ★★★★★

WELCOME TO
ST. MAARTEN/ST. MARTIN

TOP REASONS
TO GO

★ **Great Food:** The island has so many good places to dine that you could eat out for a month (or six) and never repeat a restaurant visit.

★ **Lots of Shops:** Philipsburg is one of the top shopping spots in the Caribbean and the galleries and boutiques of Marigot and Grand Case bring a touch of France.

★ **Beaches Large and Small:** Thirty-seven picture-perfect beaches are spread out across the island; some are clothing-optional.

★ **Sports Galore:** The wide range of land and water sports adventures will satisfy almost any need and give you the perfect excuse to try everything from ATVs to ziplines.

★ **Variety of Nightlife:** After-dark entertainment options include shows, lounges, discos, beach bars, and casinos.

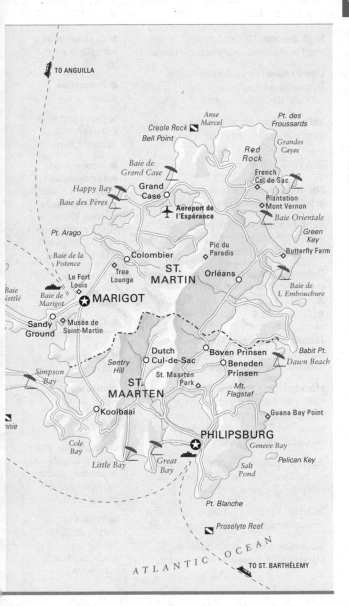

TO ANGUILLA

Anse Marcel

Creole Rock
Bell Point

Pt. des Froussards

Red Rock

Grandes Cayes

Baie de Grand Case

French Cul de Sac

Happy Bay
Baie des Pères

Grand Case

Plantation Mont Vernon

Aeroport de l'Espérance

Baie Orientale

Pt. Arago

Green Key

Baie de la Potence

Colombier

Pic du Paradis

Butterfly Farm

Tree Lounge

ST. MARTIN

Orléans

Le Fort Louis

Baie Nettlé

Baie de Marigot

MARIGOT

Baie de L. Embouchure

Sandy Ground

Musée de Saint-Martin

Dutch Cul-de-Sac

Boven Prinsen

Babit Pt.

Sentry Hill

Beneden Prinsen

Dawn Beach

Simpson Bay

St. Maarten Park

ST. MAARTEN

Mt. Flagstaf

nnie

Koolbaai

Guana Bay Point

Cole Bay

PHILIPSBURG

Geneve Bay

Little Bay

Great Bay

Pelican Key

Salt Pond

Pt. Blanche

Proselyte Reef

ATLANTIC OCEAN

TO ST. BARTHÉLEMY

ISLAND SNAPSHOT

WHEN TO GO

High Season: December–April is the most fashionable and expensive season.

Low Season: From August to late October the weather is hot and humid, with the risk of hurricanes.

Value Season: Hotel prices are lower from late April to July and in late fall.

WAYS TO SAVE

Eat at lolos. SXM's open-air roadside grills offer delicious food on the cheap.

Rent a condo. Condos can provide many of the same amenities as pricey villas, including kitchens.

Cross the border. Almost everything is cheaper on the Dutch side.

BIG EVENTS

January–February: The French side's Carnival is a pre-Lenten bash of costume parades, music, and feasts.

March: The Dutch side hosts the Heineken Regatta, with as many as 200 sailboats competing from around the world. The SXM Music Festival is held at venues all over the island.

April: Carnival takes place after Easter on the Dutch side with a parade, music competitions, and concerts.

July: On the French side, celebrations commemorate Bastille Day on July 14.

November: Both sides celebrate St. Maarten's/St. Martin's Day November 11.

AT A GLANCE

- **Capital:** Phillipsburg (D); Marigot (F)

- **Population:** 83,900

- **Currency:** Netherlands Antilles florin (D); euro (F)

- **Money:** ATMs are common and dispense U.S. dollars, Netherlands Antilles Florins or euros; credit cards and U.S. dollars widely accepted.

- **Language:** Dutch, French, English

- **Country Code:** 1 721 (D); 1 590 (F)

- **Emergencies:** 911 (D); 17 (F)

- **Driving:** On the right

- **Electricity:** Plugs are U.S. standard two- and three-prong (D) and European standard with two round prongs (F)

- **Time:** EST during daylight saving time; one hour ahead otherwise

St. Maarten/St. Martin is unique among Caribbean destinations. The 37-square-mile (96-square-km) island is a seamless place (there are no border gates), but it is governed by two nations—the Netherlands and France—and has residents from more than 100 countries. A call from the Dutch side to the French is an international call, currencies are different, electric current differs, and even the vibe is different. Only the island of Hispaniola, which encompasses Haiti and the Dominican Republic, is in a similar position in the Caribbean.

Happily for Americans, who make up the majority of visitors to St. Maarten/St. Martin, English works in both nations. Dutch St. Maarten might feel particularly comfortable for Americans: the prices are a bit lower (not to mention in U.S. dollars), the big hotels have casinos, and there is more nightlife. Huge cruise ships disgorge masses of shoppers into the Philipsburg shopping area at midmorning, when roads may become congested. But once you pass the meandering, unmarked border to the French side, you find a hint of the south of France: quiet countryside, fine cuisine, and in Marigot, a walkable harbor area with outdoor cafés, a great outdoor market, and some shops to explore.

Almost 4,000 years ago, it was salt and not tourism that drove this little island's economy. The Arawak people, the island's first known inhabitants, prospered until the warring Caribs invaded, adding the peaceful Arawaks to their list of conquests. Columbus spotted the isle on November 11, 1493, and named it after St. Martin (whose feast day is November 11), but it wasn't populated by Europeans until the 17th century, when it was claimed by the Dutch, French, and Spanish. The Dutch and French finally joined forces to claim the island in 1644, and the Treaty of Concordia partitioned the territory in 1648. According to legend the border was drawn along the line where a French man and a Dutch man, walking from opposite coasts, met.

Both sides of the island offer a touch of European culture along with a lot of laid-back Caribbean ambience. Water sports both serene and extreme abound—diving, snorkeling, sailing, wind-surfing, kitesurfing, ziplining, and even hover-boarding. With soft trade winds cooling the subtropical climate, it's easy to while away the day relaxing on one of the 37 beaches, strolling Philips-burg's boardwalk, shopping along Philipsburg's Front Street or the harbors of Marigot. Although luck is an important commodity at St. Maarten's dozen or so casinos, chance plays no part in finding a good meal at the hundreds of excellent restaurants or after-dark fun in the subtle to sizzling nightlife.

When cruise ships are in port on the Dutch side (there can be as many as nine at once), shopping areas are crowded and traffic moves at a snail's pace. Instead spend those days at your resort or one of the full-service beach clubs, or out on the water, and plan shopping excursions for the early morning or at cocktail hour, after "rush hour" traffic calms down. Still, these are minor inconveniences compared with the feel of the sand between your toes or the breeze through your hair, gourmet food sating your appetite, and being able to crisscross freely between two nations on one island.

Planning

Getting Here and Around

AIR

More than 20 carriers fly to the island. There are nonstop flights from Atlanta (Delta, seasonal), Boston (JetBlue, seasonal), Char-lotte (American), Miami/Ft. Lauderdale (American and JetBlue), New York–JFK (American, Delta, JetBlue), Newark, Chicago, and Dulles (United, seasonal), Ft. Lauderdale (JetBlue, Spirit), Orlando (Frontier), and Philadelphia (American). Nonstop flights also arrive from both Paris (Air France) and Amsterdam (KLM) as well as Pan-ama (Copa, which has many connections from and to the United States). There are also direct flights from Montreal and Toronto and some nonstop charter flights (including some from Boston). You can also connect in San Juan on Seabourne and Winair, the St. Maarten–based local carrier. Many smaller Caribbean-based airlines, including Air Caraïbes, Air Antilles, Anguilla Air Services, Caribbean Airlines, Air Sunshine, St. Barth Commuter, and Winair (Windward Islands Airways), offer service from other islands in the Caribbean.

AIRPORTS Aéroport de L'Espérance (SFG). ⊠ *Rte. de l'Espérance, Grand Case* ☎ *0590/27–11–00* ⊕ *www.saintmartin-airport.com.* **Princess Juliana International Airport** (SXM). ☎ *721/546–7542* ⊕ *www.sxmairport.com.*

BOAT AND FERRY

You can take ferries to St. Barth (45–60 minutes, €55–€90 from the French side, though you can pay in dollars or $85–$115 from the Dutch side); to Anguilla (25 minutes, €25 from the French side); and to Saba (one to two hours, $90–$100 from the Dutch side).

CONTACTS Aqua Mania Adventures. ⊠ *Simpson Bay Resort Marina Plaza, Simpson Bay* ☎ *721/544–2640* ⊕ *www.stmaarten-activities. com.* **Calypso Charters.** ⊠ *Blowing Point Ferry Terminal, Blowing Point, for ferry service between St. Barth, Anguilla, and St. Maarten/Martin* ☎ *264/462-8504.* **Great Bay Express.** ⊠ *Bobby's Marina Village, Philipsburg* ☎ *721/542–0032 Dutch side* ⊕ *www. greatbayexpress.com.* **Link Ferries.** ⊠ *Marigot* ☎ *264/772–4901* ⊕ *www.linkferry.com.* **Makana Ferry Service.** ☎ *721/543-8915* ⊕ *www.makanaferryservice.com.* **Voyager.** ⊠ *Marigot* ☎ *0590/87– 10–68* ⊕ *www.voy12.com.*

CAR

It's easy to get around the island by car. Virtually all roads are paved and in generally good condition. However, they can be crowded, especially during high season; you might experience traffic jams, particularly around Marigot around noon and Simpson Bay from 3 pm. Be alert for occasional potholes and unpainted speed bumps (small signs warn you), as well as the island tradition of stopping in the middle of the road to chat with a friend or yield to someone entering traffic. Be aware that there is no stopping in a roundabout to allow someone to enter the roundabout. Few roads are identified by name or number, but most have signs indicating the destination. Driving is on the right. There are gas stations all over the island, but gas tends to be cheaper on the French side.

Car Rentals: You can book a car at Princess Juliana International SXM Airport, where all major rental companies have booths, but it is often *much* cheaper to reserve a car in advance from home. That's also an especially wise move in high season when some companies may run out of cars. A shuttle to the rental-car companies' lots is provided. Rates are among the best in the Caribbean, as little as $25–$40 per day in low season, but at least $240/week, and up, in high season. You can also rent a car on the French side, but this rarely makes sense for Americans because of the exchange rates.

CAR-RENTAL CONTACTS Avis. ✉ *Airport Rd., Simpson Bay*
☎ *888/777–2847, 721/545-2847* ⊕ *www.avis.com.* **Budget.**
☎ *800/472–3325, 721/587–2847* ⊕ *www.sxmbudget.com.* **Dollar/
Thrifty Car Rental.** ✉ *102 Airport Rd.* ☎ *721/545–2393* ⊕ *www.dol-
larthriftysxm.com.* **Empress Rent-a-Car.** ☎ *721/545–2062* ⊕ *www.
empressrentacar.com.*

TAXI

There is a government-sponsored taxi dispatcher at the airport
and the harbor. Posted fares are for one or two people. Add $5
for each additional person, half price for kids. The first bag is free;
after that it's $1 per bag. It costs about $18 from the airport to
Philipsburg or Marigot, and about $30 to Dawn Beach. After 10
pm fares go up 25%, and after midnight 50%. Licensed drivers
can be identified by the "taxi" or new "T" license plate on the
Dutch side and the TXI license plate on the French side. Avoid any
uninsured illegal cabs that may appear; they have no such plates,
and police have been cracking down on them across the island.
Fixed fares apply from Juliana International Airport and the Marigot ferry to hotels around the island.

TAXI CONTACTS Juliana Airport Taxi Dispatch. ☎ *721/542–
1681* ⊕ *www.sxmairporttaxis.com.* **Marigot Taxi Dispatch.**
☎ *0590/87–56–54.*

Sights

The best way to explore St. Maarten/St. Martin is by car. Though
sometimes congested, especially around Philipsburg and Marigot,
the roads are fairly good, though narrow and winding, with some
speed bumps, potholes, roundabouts, and an occasional wan-
dering goat herd or stray oxen. Few roads are marked with their
names, but destination signs are somewhat common. Besides,
the island is so small that it's hard to get really lost.

If you're spending a few days, get to know the area with a
scenic loop around the island. Be sure to pack a towel and some
water shoes, a hat, sunglasses, and sunblock. Head up the east
shoreline from Philipsburg, and follow the signs to Dawn Beach
and Oyster Pond. The road winds past soaring hills, turquoise
waters, quaint West Indian houses, and wonderful views of St.
Barth. As you cross over to the French side, keep following the
road toward Orient Bay, the St-Tropez of the Caribbean. Continue
to Anse Marcel, Grand Case, and Marigot. From Marigot, the
flat neighboring island of Anguilla is visible. Completing the loop
through Sandy Ground and the French lowlands brings you past
Cupecoy Beach, through Maho and Simpson Bay, where Saba

looms on the southern horizon, and back over the mountain road into Philipsburg. A few have called it "the Great Circle Route," for good reason.

Beaches

For such a small island, St. Maarten/St. Martin has a wide array of beaches, from the long expanse of Baie Orientale on the French side to powdery-soft Mullet Bay on the Dutch side.

Several of the best Dutch-side beaches are developed and have large-scale resorts. But others, including Simpson Bay and Cupecoy, have comparatively little development. You'll sometimes find vendors or beach bars to rent chairs and umbrellas (but not always).

Almost all of the French-side beaches, whether busy Baie Orientale or less busy Baie des Pères (Friar's Bay), have beach clubs and restaurants. For about $20–$25 a couple you get two chaises (*transats*) and an umbrella (*parasol*) for the day, not to mention chair-side service for drinks and food. Only some beaches have bathrooms and showers, so if that is your preference, inquire.

Warm surf and a gentle breeze can be found at the island's 37 beaches, though breezes are generally a bit stronger on the windward Eastern shore. Every beach is open to the public. Try several. Each is unique: some bustling and some bare, some refined and some rocky, some good for snorkeling and some for sunning. Whatever your fancy, it's here, including a clothing-optional beach at the south end of beautiful Baie Orientale (Orient Beach). And several of the island's gems don't have big hotels lining their shores. Many beaches have chair rental concessions and beach bars, too.

■ TIP→ **Petty theft from cars in beach parking lots occasionally happens. Leave nothing in your parked car, not even in the glove compartment or especially the trunk.**

Restaurants

Although most people come to St. Maarten/St. Martin for sun and fun, they leave praising the incredible cuisine available on both sides of the island. On an isle that covers only 37 square miles (96 square km), there are literally hundreds of restaurants.

Some of the best restaurants are in Grand Case (on the French side), but many other fine dining restaurants now are in Simpson

Bay and Porto Cupecoy, both on the Dutch side. Don't limit your culinary adventures to one area. Try the hopping upscale restaurants of Cupecoy, the tourist-friendly low-key eateries of Simpson Bay, and the many *lolos* (roadside barbecue stands) throughout. Loyalists on both "sides" will cheerfully try to steer you to their favorites. Do remember that some French-side restaurants may still offer a one-to-one exchange rate if you use cash.

During high season, it's essential to make reservations. Sometimes you can make them the same day. Dutch-side restaurants may include a 15% service charge, so check your bill before tipping. On the French side, service is usually included (worth checking, here, too), but it is customary to leave 5%–10% extra. Don't leave tips on your credit card—it's customary to tip in cash. A taxi is probably the easiest solution to the parking problems in Grand Case, Marigot, and Philipsburg. Grand Case has two pay lots—each costs several dollars—at each end of the main boulevard, and there's one well-lit free lot toward the northern end of town, which usually fills up by 8 pm. Restaurants will be happy to call you a cab to return at the end of the meal.

What to Wear: Although appropriate dining attire ranges from swimsuits to sport jackets, casual dress is usually just fine. A nice shirt and pants or a skirt will take you almost anywhere. Jeans are fine in less formal eateries.

Restaurant prices are the average cost of a main course at dinner or, if dinner is not served, at lunch. Restaurant reviews have been shortened. For full information, visit Fodors.com.

Hotels and Resorts

The island, though small, is well developed—some say overdeveloped—and offers a wide range of lodging. The larger resorts and time-shares are on the Dutch side; the French side has more intimate properties. Just keep in mind that the popular restaurants around Grand Case, on the French side, are a long drive from most Dutch-side hotels—but there are now lots of great restaurants in Simpson Bay and at Porto Cupecoy. French-side hotels charge in euros. Be wary of very low–price alternatives, short-term housing for temporary workers, or properties used by very low-end tour companies. Some locations very close to the airport can be a bit noisy.

Resorts and Time-Shares: Virtually every SXM time-share and resort has been rebuilt better and stronger in the past few years due to hurricanes. There are several resorts with all-inclusive options, but before you lock yourself into a meal plan, keep in mind that restaurants at all price points are easily accessible (and that opting for an all-inclusive resort could deprive you of some seriously memorable dining experiences).

Small Inns: Small guesthouses and inns can be found on both sides of the island. It's worth considering these, especially if you are not the big-resort type. Several are quite modern and attractive, and located beachfront.

Villas and Condos: Both sides of the island have hundreds of villas and condos for every conceivable budget. Some of the resorts offer villa alternatives, which make for a good compromise, and perhaps better security. In addition, many high-end condo developments offer unsold units as rentals—and some are brand-new and terrific bargains.

Hotel prices are the lowest cost of a standard double room in high season. Hotel reviews have been shortened. For full information, visit Fodors.com.

What It Costs in U.S. Dollars

	$	$$	$$$	$$$$
RESTAURANTS				
	under $12	$12–$20	$21–$30	over $30
HOTELS				
	under $275	$275–$375	$376–$475	over $475

St. Maarten/St. Martin accommodations range from modern megaresorts to condos, villas, and stylish intimate guesthouses. On the Dutch side some hotels cater to groups, and although that's also true to some extent on the French side, you can find a larger collection of intimate accommodations there.

■TIP→ **Off-season rates (April through the beginning of December) can be as little as half the high-season rates.**

TIME-SHARE RENTALS
Time-share properties are concentrated on the Dutch side. There's no need to buy a share, as these condos are rented out by the resorts or by time-share owners themselves whenever the owners are not in residence. If you stay in one, try to avoid a sales pitch—they can last up to two hours. Some rent by the night, but there are substantial savings if you secure a weekly rate. Not all offer daily maid service.

PRIVATE VILLAS

Villas are a great lodging option, especially for families who don't need to keep the kids occupied, or for groups of friends who like hanging out together. Since these are for the most part free-standing houses, their greatest advantage is privacy. Properties are scattered throughout the island, often in gated communities or on secluded roads. Although a few have bare-bones furnishings, most are quite luxurious, sometimes with gyms, theaters, game rooms, and several different pools. There are private chefs, gardeners, maids, and other staffers to care for both the villa and its occupants.

Villas are secured through rental companies. They offer weekly prices that range from reasonable to more than many people make in a year. Check around, as prices for the same property vary from agent to agent. Rental companies usually provide airport transfers and concierge service, and for an extra fee will even stock your refrigerator.

HomeAway

This listing service is the world's leading vacation rentals marketplace. To rent a condo, you contact the owner directly. ⊕ *www. homeaway.com.*

Island Properties

This company's properties are scattered around the island. ⊠ *62 Welfare Rd., Simpson Bay* ☎ *721/544–4580, 866/978–0470 in U.S.* ⊕ *www.remaxislandproperties.com.*

Island Real Estate Team / IRE Vacations

Island Real Estate Team and its IRE Vacations division offer both sales and rentals of villas, condominiums, businesses, property, and more on both the French and Dutch sides of SXM. ⊠ *91-b Welfare Rd., Simpson Bay* ☎ *721/544–4240* ⊕ *www.ireteam.com.*

Jennifer's Vacation Villas

Jennifer's specializes in vacation villas across the island, handling both short- and long-term rentals as well as villa purchases. ⊠ *Plaza del Lago, Welfare Rd., Simpson Bay* ☎ *721/544—3107, 631/546–7345* ✎ *www.jennifersvacationvillas.com.*

St. Maarten Sotheby's International Realty

St. Maarten Sotheby's International Realty sells and rents luxury villas, many in gated communities. ⊠ *One Cupecoy, 1 Niger Rd., Cupecoy* ☎ *721/545–3626, 213/805–0840* ⊕ *www.stmartinsir. com.*

Villas of Distinction

This company rents villas worldwide. ☎ *800/289–0900 in U.S.* ⊕ *www.villasofdistinction.com.*

WIMCO

This outfit has more hotel, villa, apartment, and condo listings in the Caribbean than many, and it has over 30 years of experience. ☎ *401/239–0319 in U.S., 888888/997–3970 toll-free* ⊕ *www. wimco.com.*

Nightlife

St. Maarten has lots of evening and late-night action. To find out what's going on, pick up *St. Maarten Nights,* distributed free in the tourist office and hotels, or the Thursday edition of *The Daily Herald,* the Dutch-side newspaper. The glossy *Discover St. Martin/ St. Maarten* magazine, also free, has articles on island history and on the newest shops, discos, and restaurants.

The island's many casinos are only on the Dutch side. All have craps, blackjack, roulette, and slot machines. You must be 18 or older to gamble. Dress is casual (but not bathing suits or skimpy beachwear). Most casinos are in hotels, but there are also some that are free-standing; all are open to the public.

Shopping

Shopaholics are drawn to the array of stores—and jewelry, watches, and high-end handbags in particular are big business on both sides of the island, with the greatest concentration of jewelers on Front Street in Philipsburg. Start at the center of town near the historic Court House on Front Street. Many of the best stores are closest to the Court House. In addition, duty-free shops can offer substantial savings—about 15% to 30% below U.S. and Canadian prices—on cameras, liquor, cigars, and designer clothing, but prices are not always better, so make sure you know U.S. prices beforehand—and bargain hard. Stick with the big vendors that advertise in the tourist press to get the best quality. Be alert for idlers: they've been known on rare occassions to snatch unwatched purses. .

Prices are in dollars on the Dutch side, and in euros on the French side. More bargains are to be had on the Dutch side; prices on the French side may be higher than back home, and prices in euros don't help. Merchandise may not be from the newest collections, especially with regard to clothing, but there are items available on the French side that are not available on the Dutch side.

Visitor Information

CONTACTS St Maarten Tourist Information Bureau. ☎ *721/549–0200* ⊕ *www.vacationstmaarten.com*. **St Martin Office de Tourisme.** ✉ *Rte. de Sandy Ground, Marigot* ⊕ *www.st-martin.org*.

Weddings

There's a three-day waiting period on the Dutch side—but wait, it's worse: paperwork may take several weeks to process, so be sure your venue or wedding planner has a couple of months (preferably) to get everything done for you. Yes, you can do a memorable tropical wedding on a beach, but no, you can't possibly do it tomorrow. Getting married on the French side is not a viable option because of long residency requirements.

St. Maarten (Dutch Side)

Philipsburg

The capital of Dutch St. Maarten stretches about a mile (1½ km) along an isthmus between Great Bay and the Salt Pond and has five parallel streets. Most of the village's dozens of shops and restaurants are on Front Street, narrow and cobblestone, closest to Great Bay. It can be congested when cruise ships are in port because of its many duty-free shops and several casinos, but on the busiest days, it's closed off to vehicular traffic so Front Street becomes a pleasant pedestrian mall. Little lanes called *steegjes* connect Front Street with Back Street, where locals shop for clothes and sundries. Along the beach is a ½-mile-long (1-km-long) boardwalk with restaurants, souvenir shops, and beach concessions where you can rent chairs and umbrellas for about $20, sometimes with cold drinks included. There are many Wi-Fi hot spots. The boardwalk—technically called the "Great Bay Beach Promenade"—is being further extended at its eastern end all the way to the Cruise & Cargo Facilities, which will make for a much more scenic and enjoyable walk from the port to downtown Philipsburg.

Sights

Rainforest Adventures St. Maarten

AMUSEMENT PARK/CARNIVAL | FAMILY | This eco-adventure park, designed so it would minimally impact the island's nature, offers 360-degree views of the island and adrenaline pumping rides. Nose around the Emilio Wilson museum and learn about the island's history before you take the chairlift all the way to the top of Sentry Hill to the sky explorer, a wooden deck from which you can enjoy the most incredible views of the island. Get a cold beverage at the Sky Bar and work up the nerve to go down the hill with either the Sentry Hill zipline, the schooner ride or–if you dare–the famous Flying Dutchman, also known as the steepest zipline in the world. After all the excitement, treat yourself to a nice lunch at Emilio's restaurant located on the property. ⊠ *Rockland Estates, 59 L.B. Scott Rd., Philipsburg* ☎ *721/543–1135* ⊕ *www.rainforestadventure.com/st-maarten* ⚟ *From $52* ⊗ *Closed Fri.*

St. Maarten Museum

HISTORY MUSEUM | Hosting rotating cultural exhibits that address the history, industry, geology, and archaeology of the island, the museum contains artifacts ranging from Arawak pottery shards to objects salvaged from the wreck of HMS *Proselyte*. An interesting exhibit about hurricanes focuses on Hurricane Luis, which devastated the island in 1995. There is a good reference and video library as well. ⊠ *7 Front St., Philipsburg* ☎ *721/542–4917* ⊕ *www.sintmaartenmuseum.org* ⚟ *Free, but donations are welcome.*

★ Yoda Guy Movie Exhibit

OTHER MUSEUM | FAMILY | This odd-sounding exhibit is actually a nonprofit museum run by Nick Maley, a movie-industry artist who was involved in the creation of Yoda and other icons. You can learn how the artist worked while enjoying the models and memorabilia on display—a must-see for *Star Wars* fans but of interest to most movie buffs. Maley is often on-hand and is happy to answer questions as time allows, and to autograph souvenirs for sale. ⊠ *19a Front St., Philipsburg* ☎ *721/542–4009*.

Beaches

Great Bay

BEACH | This bustling white-sand beach curves around Philipsburg just behind Front Street, making it easy to find. Here you'll find boutiques, eateries, a pleasant boardwalk, and rental chairs and umbrellas. Often busy with cruise-ship passengers, the beach is best west of Captain Hodge Pier or around Antoine

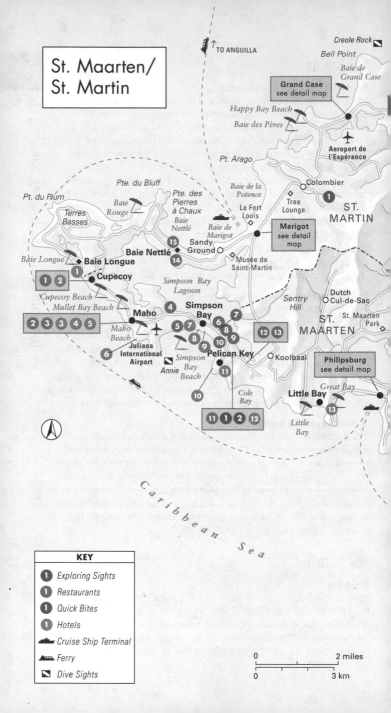

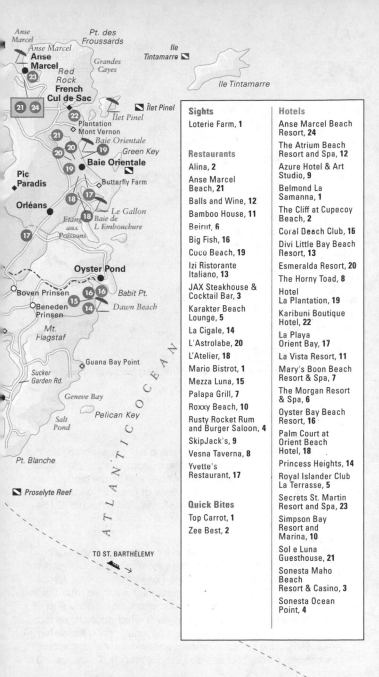

Sights	Hotels
Loterie Farm, **1**	Anse Marcel Beach Resort, **24**
	The Atrium Beach Resort and Spa, **12**
Restaurants	Azure Hotel & Art Studio, **9**
Alina, **2**	Belmond La Samanna, **1**
Anse Marcel Beach, **21**	The Cliff at Cupecoy Beach, **2**
Balls and Wine, **12**	Coral Beach Club, **15**
Bamboo House, **11**	Divi Little Bay Beach Resort, **13**
Beirut, **6**	Esmeralda Resort, **20**
Big Fish, **16**	The Horny Toad, **8**
Coco Beach, **19**	Hotel La Plantation, **19**
Izi Ristorante Italiano, **13**	Karibuni Boutique Hotel, **22**
JAX Steakhouse & Cocktail Bar, **3**	La Playa Orient Bay, **17**
Karakter Beach Lounge, **5**	La Vista Resort, **11**
La Cigale, **14**	Mary's Boon Beach Resort & Spa, **7**
L'Astrolabe, **20**	The Morgan Resort & Spa, **6**
L'Atelier, **18**	Oyster Bay Beach Resort, **16**
Mario Bistrot, **1**	Palm Court at Orient Beach Hotel, **18**
Mezza Luna, **15**	Princess Heights, **14**
Palapa Grill, **7**	Royal Islander Club La Terrasse, **5**
Roxxy Beach, **10**	Secrets St. Martin Resort and Spa, **23**
Rusty Rocket Rum and Burger Saloon, **4**	Simpson Bay Resort and Marina, **10**
SkipJack's, **9**	Sol e Luna Guesthouse, **21**
Vesna Taverna, **8**	Sonesta Maho Beach Resort & Casino, **3**
Yvette's Restaurant, **17**	Sonesta Ocean Point, **4**
Quick Bites	
Top Carrot, **1**	
Zee Best, **2**	

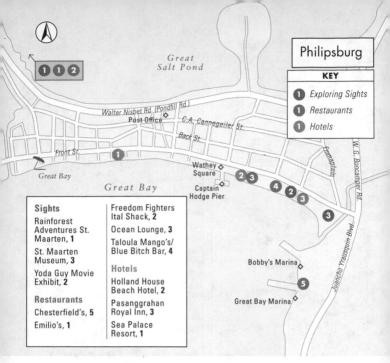

Philipsburg

KEY

1 *Exploring Sights*

1 *Restaurants*

1 *Hotels*

Sights

Rainforest Adventures St. Maarten, **1**

St. Maarten Museum, **3**

Yoda Guy Movie Exhibit, **2**

Restaurants

Chesterfield's, **5**

Emilio's, **1**

Freedom Fighters Ital Shack, **2**

Ocean Lounge, **3**

Taloula Mango's/ Blue Bitch Bar, **4**

Hotels

Holland House Beach Hotel, **2**

Pasanggrahan Royal Inn, **3**

Sea Palace Resort, **1**

Restaurant. **Amenities:** food and drink. **Best for:** swimming; walking. ⊠ *Philipsburg.*

🍴 Restaurants

Chesterfield's

$$$ | CARIBBEAN | FAMILY | Both locals and tourists seem to love this casual restaurant at Great Bay Marina. Seafood is the main focus, but steaks, burgers, pasta, and poultry are all on the dinner menu. **Known for:** happy hour (5–7); nice views of Great Bay; lobster. ⑤ *Average main: $24* ⊠ *Great Bay Marina, Philipsburg* ☎ 721/542–3484 ⊕ *www.chesterfields.sx.*

★ Emilio's

$$$ | CARIBBEAN | FAMILY | Located in a historic sugarcane boiling house from the 1700s, St. Maarten's most talked-about fine dining experience invites you to "dine with history" on nouveau Caribbean cuisine. The award-winning restaurant is named after Emilio Wilson, who bought the plantation on which his grandparents worked and died as enslaved people and which today is the location of the restaurant and Rainforest Adventure park. **Known for:** impressive wine selection; historic atmosphere in a chic setting; exceptional menu, cocktails, and Sunday brunch. ⑤ *Average main:*

$28 ⊠ 59 L.B. Scott Rd., Philipsburg ☏ 721/522–1848 ⊕ www. emilios-sxm.com ⊗ Closed on Mon. Closed for dinner on Sun.

Freedom Fighters Ital Shack

$ | CARIBBEAN | FAMILY | Made famous by the late Anthony Bourdain after he stopped here in 2000, this local, vibrant spot on the edge of town is well-known for its colorful exterior and animated owner. Serving ital food (vegan and organic) made of strictly local ingredients from either their own land out back or from local farmers, the Ital Shack has a very loyal following. **Known for:** organic, vegan meals; colorful decor inspired by the Rastafarian belief; fresh juice made from local fruits and veggies. *$ Average main: $10 ⊠ 7 Bush Rd., Philipsburg ☏ 721/542–0055 ⊕ www.sxmfreedomfighters.com ▭ No credit cards ⊗ No breakfast and lunch Sat. Closed on Sun. ⌨ Cash only.*

Ocean Lounge

$$$$ | ECLECTIC | FAMILY | An airy modern verandah perched on the Philipsburg boardwalk gives a distinct South Beach vibe. You'll want to linger over fresh fish and steaks as you watch tourists pass by on romantic strolls by night or determined cruise-ship passengers surveying the surrounding shops by day. **Known for:** beachfront lounge; easy place to relax and people-watch; gathering place for Philipsburg movers and shakers. *$ Average main: $35 ⊠ Holland House Beach Hotel, 45 Front St., Philipsburg ☏ 721/542–2572 ⊕ www.hhbh.com.*

Taloula Mango's/Blue Bitch Bar

$$ | ECLECTIC | FAMILY | Ribs and burgers are the specialty at this casual beachfront restaurant, but Gouda cheese sticks and quesadillas, not to mention the flatbread pizza options, are not to be ignored. Opt to have lunch on the beach; beach chairs and umbrellas are complimentary with lunch and beach service is available. **Known for:** delicious tapas; beach views and people-watching; location on the Philipsburg boardwalk. *$ Average main: $19 ⊠ Sint Rose Arcade, Philipsburg ✦ Off Front St. on the boardwalk ☏ 721/542–1645 ⊕ www.bluebitchbar.com.*

Hotels

Holland House Beach Hotel

$ | HOTEL | This hotel is in an ideal location for shoppers and sun worshippers; it faces Front Street and to the rear are the boardwalk and a long stretch of Great Bay Beach. **Pros:** easy access to beach and shops; all rooms have balconies; in the heart of Philipsburg. **Cons:** no pool; getting there by car is challenging when many cruise ships visit; busy downtown location can be noisy. *$ Rooms* *from: $255* ⊠ *45 Front St., Philipsburg* ☎ *721/542–2572* ⊕ *www. hhbh.com* ⌨ *55 rooms* ⦿| *Free Breakfast.*

Pasanggrahan Royal Inn

$ | **B&B/INN** | One of the few remaining authentic West Indian properties on St. Maarten is steeped in history; in fact, the island's oldest hotel once served as the governor's mansion. **Pros:** in the heart of Philipsburg; historic; inexpensive. **Cons:** beach can be crowded; street side can be noisy; on the main drag, which can be loaded with people. ⑤ *Rooms from: $154* ⊠ *15 Front St., Philipsburg* ☎ *721/542–3588* ⊕ *www.pasanhotel.net* ⌨ *19 rooms* ⦿| *No Meals.*

Sea Palace Resort

$ | **TIMESHARE** | **FAMILY** | This hotel and time-share, which is right on the beach in Philipsburg, is painted an eye-popping shade of coral that is hard to miss. **Pros:** walking distance to shopping; fully equipped kitchens; on Great Bay beach and the Promenade (boardwalk). **Cons:** not much for kids to do; can be a bit noisy during the day due to traffic; area is crowded when cruise ships dock. ⑤ *Rooms from: $229* ⊠ *147 Front St., Philipsburg* ☎ *721/542– 2700, 866/998–5333* ⊕ *www.seapalaceresort.com* ⌨ *32 units* ⦿| *No Meals.*

Nightlife

Axum Art Café and Gallery

CAFÉS | This 1960s-style gallery and jazz café offers local cultural activities as well as live music and poetry readings. It's open Thursday, Friday, and Saturday 10–5. ⊠ *7L Front St., Philipsburg* ⊹ *Near the Guavaberry Emporium toward the east end of Front St.* ☎ *590/88–96–63 French side phone number* ⊕ *www.axumart-cafe.com.*

★ Ocean Lounge

BARS | Sip a guavaberry colada and sample tapas with your chair pointed toward the boardwalk at this popular, genuinely Caribbean venue. There's free parking for patrons until midnight; enter on Back Street, and look for the Holland House banner. ⊠ *Holland House Beach Hotel, 43 Front St., Philipsburg* ☎ *721/542–2572* ⊕ *www.hhbh.com.*

🛍 Shopping

Philipsburg's **Front Street** reinvented itself several years ago and continues to evolve. Now it's mall-like, with a redbrick walk and streets, some palm trees lining the sleek boutiques, jewelry stores, souvenir shops, and outdoor restaurants. Here and there a school or a church appears to remind visitors there's much more to this island than shopping. On Back Street, the **Philipsburg Market Place** is a daily open-air market where you can haggle over handicrafts, souvenirs, and beachwear. **Old Street,** off Front Street, has little stores, boutiques, and island mementos.

Ballerina Jewelers

JEWELRY & WATCHES | One of the most popular jewelry stores on the island, Ballerina has jewelry by Tacori and Pandora, and watches by Bell & Ross, Franck Muller, and other luxury brands. ⊠ 56 Front St., Philipsburg ☎ 721/542–4399 ⊕ www.ballerina-jewelers. com.

★ Caribbean Gems

JEWELRY & WATCHES | One of St. Maarten's oldest and most popular jewelers, Caribbean Gems has two Philipsburg locations, at both 22 and 40 Front Street, an easy walk especially for cruise ship passengers. The store features one-of-a-kind jewelry and watches in all price ranges, including many sold exclusively there. Known for impeccable customer service, Caribbean Gems has a wide selection and competitive pricing. ⊠ 22 Front St. and 40 Front St. ☎ 721/542–2176, 646/472–7996 ⊕ www.caribbeangems.com.

Guavaberry Emporium

WINE/SPIRITS | Visitors come for free samples at the small factory where the Sint Maarten Guavaberry Company sells its famous liqueur. The many versions include one made with jalapeño peppers. Check out the hand-painted bottles. The store also sells a gourmet barbecue and hot sauce collection and souvenir hats. ⊠ 8–10 Front St., Philipsburg ☎ 721/542–2965 ⊕ www.guavaberry. com.

Little Europe

JEWELRY & WATCHES | Come here to buy fine jewelry, crystal, and china; they carry many top brands. They have two stores in Philipsburg on 2 Front St. and 80 Front St., and one in Marigot on Rue de General de Gaulle. ⊠ 80 Front St., Philipsburg ☎ 721/542–4371 ⊕ www.littleeurope.com.

Oro Diamante

JEWELRY & WATCHES | Specializing in diamonds, this store carries loose diamonds, jewelry, and watches. ⊠ 62-B Front St., Philipsburg ☎ 599/543–0342, 800/764–0884 in U.S. ⊕ www.oro-diamante.com.

Shipwreck Shop

CRAFTS | With multiple SXM outlets, this chain stocks a little of everything: colorful hammocks, handmade jewelry, and local

The white sands of Cupecoy Beach border on sandstone cliffs.

guavaberry liqueur. But the main store has the largest selection. ✉ *42 Front St., Philipsburg* ☎ *721/542–2962* ⊕ *www.shipwreck-shops.com.*

★ Zhaveri Jewelers & Luxury

JEWELRY & WATCHES | A fixture on Front Street for more than 30 years, Zhaveri has a huge selection of loose diamonds, jewelry, watches, and gifts, plus designer handbags from Hugo Boss, Georgio Armani, Emporio Armani, Kartell, Furla, and Carmen Sol, as well as jewelry pieces sold nowhere else on SXM. They pay no fees to cruise lines, which makes their pricing highly competitive. ✉ *68 Front St.* ☎ *721/543–1075* ⊕ *www.zhaveri.com.*

Cupecoy

 Beaches

★ Cupecoy Beach

BEACH | Near the Dutch-French border, this highly picturesque area of sandstone cliffs, white sand, and shoreline caves is actually a string of small beaches that come and go according to the whims of the sea. The surf can be rough, and it's a steep walk down to parts of the beach. Despite some "no nudity" signs at the neighboring Shore Pointe condos, this beach has been "clothing optional" for decades—but wait until you're on the beach itself before disrobing. Friendly "Dany's Beach Bar," located at the top of the stairs to the beach, serves all kinds of drinks and snacks, and sometimes fresh Caribbean spiny lobster. It's also a superb place for meeting people who gather here from around the world. **Amenities:** food, drink; chair and umbrella rentals. **Best for:** relaxation; sunsets. ⊠ *Between Baie Longue and Mullet Bay, Cupecoy.*

★ Mullet Bay Beach

BEACH | FAMILY | Many believe that this mile-long, powdery white-sand beach behind the Mullet Bay Golf Course is the island's best. You can rent umbrellas and chairs here. Swimmers like it because the water is usually calm. Be cautious here; undertow can be challenging. Always swim with others nearby, since there are no lifeguards. The comparatively calm cove at the south end is good for kids. Listen for the "whispering pebbles" as the waves wash up. Beach bars serve lunch and cold drinks. **Amenities:** food and drink. **Best for:** families; snorkeling; swimming. ⊠ *South of Cupecoy and Northwest of the Maho area, Mullet Bay.*

 Restaurants

★ Mario Bistrot

$$$$ | ECLECTIC | FAMILY | With stunning views of the ocean, Mario Bistrot's new location at The Cliff offers incredible sunsets, a memorable atmosphere, and culinary excellence that ensures its ongoing popularity. Though the menu is in English and French, the cooking is an eclectic mix of Continental and Caribbean with a little Asian flare. **Known for:** generous portions (they happily provide take-home boxes); extraordinary desserts; culinary creativity. ⑤ *Average main: $35* ⊠ *The Cliff, Rhine Rd., Cupecoy* ☎ *721/523–2760* ⊕ *www.mariobistrot.com.*

Hotels

The Cliff at Cupecoy Beach

$$$ | APARTMENT | These luxurious, high-rise condos are rented out when the owners are not in residence; depending on the owner's personal style, they can be downright fabulous. **Pros:** great views; good for families; close to SXM airport and Maho and Porto Cupecoy restaurants. **Cons:** traffic and some nearby construction; getting to Orient Beach or Philipsburg is a chore from here; limited services. ⑤ *Rooms from: $425* ⊠ *Rhine Rd., Cupecoy* ☎ *721/546–6600, 721/520–6655* ⊕ *www.cliffsxm.com* ⇨ *72 units* ⑩ *No Meals.*

Maho

Beaches

Maho Beach

BEACH | People flock to the island's most famous beach to see dramatically low plane landings to Princess Juliana; they seem to pass just above your head. Be careful; the planes are loud and cause strong wind. Standing under the jet blast directly behind the plane can be dangerous and is not advised. Alternatively, you can watch from a more comfortable distance at one of two bars on either side of the beach or at the nearby Sonesta Ocean Point or Sunset Bar and Grill. **Amenities:** food and drink **Best for:** walking; windsurfing ⊠ *Maho Reef.*

Restaurants

★ Alina

$$$ | **JAPANESE FUSION** | Located above Casino Royale in the heart of the Maho entertainment area, Alina is the island's latest Japanese restaurant from the inspiring mind of expert Chef Ken. The restaurant is popular not only for the delectable Japanese dishes infused with local flavors, but also for the views from its open design. **Known for:** creative sushi rolls like the curry lobster roll; trendy atmosphere; multi-course omakase. $ *Average main: $30* ⊠ *Above Casino Royale, 1 Rhine Rd., Maho Reef* ☎ *721/587–8858* ⊕ *www.alinarestaurant.com* ⊗ *Closed Sun.*

JAX Steakhouse & Cocktail Bar

$$$$ | **STEAKHOUSE** | Diners have been flocking to JAX for Certified Angus beef steaks since the restaurant opened in 2019. The attractive ambience and great service are a tribute to the owner's years of experience as a restaurateur on the island. **Known for:** great ambience and service to match; central location in Maho; superior cocktails and quality steaks. $ *Average main: $39* ⊠ *Sonesta Maho Resort, 1 Rhine Rd., Maho Reef* ☎ *721/588–8884* ⊗ *No lunch.*

Hotels

★ The Morgan Resort & Spa

$$$ | **RESORT** | This boutique resort next to popular Maho Beach opened its doors in 2021 to rave reviews; the majority of its 124 rooms overlook the exceptional beach-style infinity pool below. **Pros:** pool with swim-up bar and cabanas; complimentary airport shuttle; great location near bars and restaurants. **Cons:** noise from

planes at adjacent airport can be heard throughout the hotel; no beach; rooms are rather simple for the price you pay. ⑤ *Rooms from: $449* ✉ *2 Beacon Hill Rd., Simpson Bay* ☎ *833/966–7426 in U.S., 721/545–4000* ⊕ *www.themorganresort.com* ⇄ *124 rooms* ⑩ *No Meals.*

Royal Islander Club La Terrasse

$$ | TIMESHARE | FAMILY | This smaller and somewhat nicer sister time-share resort to the Royal Islander Club La Plage is right across the street and shares many of the same amenities, including the larger resort's beach. **Pros:** in a hip area, near restaurants and bars; suites have nice views; convenient underground parking. **Cons:** because this is a time-share, rooms can be hard to book during peak periods; proximity to airport means it's sometimes noisy here; not on the beach. ⑤ *Rooms from: $309* ✉ *1 Rhine Rd., Maho Reef* ☎ *721/545–2388* ⊕ *www.royalislander.com* ⇄ *76 units* ⑩ *No Meals.*

Sonesta Maho Beach Resort & Casino

$$$ | RESORT | FAMILY | The island's largest hotel, which is on Maho Beach and typically caters to big groups, isn't luxurious or fancy, but it's a vibrant, attractive property. **Pros:** family-friendly; views of landing planes at nearby airport; nonstop activities. **Cons:** not for a quiet getaway; resort does not have a beach but is just steps aways from one; large resort, not remotely intimate. ⑤ *Rooms from: $468* ✉ *1 Rhine Rd., Maho Reef* ☎ *721/545–2115* ⊕ *www. sonesta.com/mahobeach* ⇄ *420 rooms* ⑩ *All-Inclusive.*

★ Sonesta Ocean Point

$$$$ | RESORT | The roomy suites in this sophisticated, luxurious enclave are some of the very best accommodations on the island. **Pros:** brand-new comfortable rooms; great design; private dining. **Cons:** proximity to airport gives you a lot of chances to watch the dramatic plane landings, but it can be noisy during takeoffs; fairly long walk to all the Maho-area restaurants and bars (golf carts available); access is through the Sonesta Maho complex. ⑤ *Rooms from: $880* ✉ *14 A Rhine Rd., Maho Reef* ☎ *721/545–3100* ⊕ *www.sonesta.com/oceanpoint* ⇄ *130 rooms* ⑩ *All-Inclusive.*

Nightlife

Casino Royale

THEMED ENTERTAINMENT | Casino Royale boasts more than 21,000 square feet of gaming and is home to the biggest theater on the island. With an amplitude of tables and slot machines, a free tiered Players Club membership, a private high-roller area, a new

Sportsbook with self-service kiosks, free Vegas-style production shows weekly, a VIP Lounge, and more, it is St. Maarten's top-rated casino. ⊠ *Sonesta Maho Beach Resort & Casino, 1 Rhine Rd., Maho Reef* ☎ *721/545–2590* ⊕ *www.playmaho.com.*

Mimosa Skylounge

BARS | After dinner at Alina, take the stairs to the top floor to Mimosa Skylounge. This rooftop cocktail lounge offers 180-degree views of the Maho area, artful concoctions by expert mixologists, and music by renowned local and international DJs. ⊠ *Above Casino Royale, 1 Rhine Rd., Maho Reef* ☎ *721/588–9988* ⊕ *www. mimosa-skylounge.com* ☉ *Closed Sun.*

Sunset Bar and Grill

BARS | This popular plane spotting bar and restaurant near the ocean edge of the Princess Juliana International Airport runway has a relaxed, anything-goes atmosphere. Watch big planes fly very low over your head a few seconds before landing, while you enjoy a BBC (Bailey's banana colada), or a bucket of beers. Bring your camera for stunning photos, but expect a high noise level. Note: drinks here can be quite pricey, and it is very busy when cruise ships are in port. There's live music on Sunday and occasionally on weeknights. ⊠ *Maho Beach, Beacon Hill # 2, Maho Reef* ☎ *721/545–2084* ⊕ *www.facebook.com/ SunsetBeachBarSXM.*

Oyster Pond

 Beaches

Dawn Beach

BEACH | True to its name, this is a great place to be at sunrise with your camera. Located on the Atlantic side of Oyster Pond, just south of the French border, it's a first-class beach for sunning and snorkeling, but the winds and rough water mean only strong swimmers should attempt to take a dip (there are no lifeguards). It's not usually crowded, and there are some good restaurants in the area. Locals often fish here in early mornings or evenings—as do brown pelicans. To find the beach, follow the signs to Oyster Bay Beach Resort, Big Fish Restaurant, or Coral Beach Club. **Amenities:** food and drink. **Best for:** snorkeling (particularly at the northern end); sunrise. ⊠ *South of Oyster Pond, Dawn Beach.*

Restaurants

★ Big Fish

$$$ | ECLECTIC | Big portions of fresh-caught fish, sushi, and steaks are served in a modern, Miami Beach atmosphere. The service is friendly and attentive. **Known for:** spicy Hurricane shrimp; creative cocktails; South Beach vibes. $ *Average main: $28* ⊠ *14 Emerald Merit Rd., Oyster Pond* ☎ *721/543–6288.*

🛏 Hotels

★ Coral Beach Club

$$$$ | RESORT | The luxurious private villas in this condo-style complex are right on the ocean or overlooking Oyster Pond. **Pros:** attention to detail; private plunge pool; private parking and use of Oyster Bay Resort amenities. **Cons:** isolated location; car needed if you want to see more of the island; expensive. $ *Rooms from: $950* ⊠ *3 Emerald Merit Rd., Oyster Pond* ☎ *866/978–7278 toll free, 721/543–6303* ⊕ *www.coralbeach-club.com* ⇆ *24 villas* ❦ *No Meals.*

Oyster Bay Beach Resort

$$ | RESORT | FAMILY | Jutting out into the Atlantic and Oyster Pond, this condo/time-share resort sits overlooking Dawn Beach and is convenient to groceries and restaurants; it appeals to those who want a relaxing atmosphere without being too far from everything else. **Pros:** lots of activities; nightly entertainment; infinity pool. **Cons:** need a car to get around; older units are smaller than new units; isolated location. $ *Rooms from: $315* ⊠ *10 Emerald Merit Rd., Oyster Pond* ☎ *888/784–6685 Toll free, 721/543–6040* ⊕ *www.OBBR.com* ⇆ *182 units* ❦ *No Meals.*

Princess Heights

$ | HOTEL | Perched on a hill hundreds of feet above the Atlantic, spacious suites offer privacy, luxury, and white-balustrade balconies with a smashing view of St. Barth. **Pros:** away from the crowds; friendly staff; gorgeous vistas. **Cons:** numerous steps to climb in the older building; not easy to find; not on the beach and need a car to get around. $ *Rooms from: $225* ⊠ *156 Oyster Pond Rd., Oyster Pond* ☎ *721/543–6906, 800/881–1744* ⊕ *www. princessheights.com* ⇆ *51 suites* ❦ *No Meals.*

Pelican Key

Hotels

The Atrium Beach Resort and Spa

$ | **RESORT** | **FAMILY** | Lush tropical foliage in the glassed-in lobby—hence the name—makes a great first impression at this good base for island explorations. **Pros:** family-friendly environment; short walk to restaurants and close to the beach; free shuttle to Philipsburg. **Cons:** neighborhood is crowded; taxes and service charges add a whopping 25% to basic rates; some rooms lack private balconies. $ Rooms from: $227 ⊠ 6 Billy Folly Rd., Pelican Key ☎ 721/544-2126, 888/992–8748 ⊕ theatriumresort.com ⇌ 87 rooms ⍾ No Meals.

La Vista Resort

$ | **TIMESHARE** | **FAMILY** | Hibiscus and bougainvillea line brick walkways that connect the bungalows and beachfront suites of this intimate and friendly, family-owned time-share resort perched at the foot of Pelican Key. The accommodations, which have completed renovations, are beautifully furnished and have small bathrooms, but the balconies have awesome views. **Pros:** close to restaurants and bars; nearest good beach is at Simpson Bay Resort, very walkable; centrally located. **Cons:** beach is a bit rocky; nothing fancy; no-frills furnishings. $ Rooms from: $205 ⊠ 53 Billy Folly Rd., Pelican Key ☎ 721/544–3005 ⊕ www.lavistaresort.com ⇌ 50 units ⍾ No Meals.

★ Simpson Bay Resort and Marina

$ | **RESORT** | **FAMILY** | Tucked away on Pelican Key, Simpson Bay Resort borders both the bay and the ocean, giving you a front-row seat for island sunsets from your terrace. **Pros:** family-friendly resort on the beach; close to restaurants and nightlife options; close to SXM airport. **Cons:** busy area; capitals are each at least 20 minutes away in perfect conditions; housekeeping service only weekly. $ Rooms from: $208 ⊠ 7 Billy Folly Rd., Pelican Key ☎ 888/721–4407, 954/736–5807 ⊕ www.simpsonbayresort.com ⇌ 355 units ⍾ No Meals.

Nightlife

Buccaneer Beach Bar

BARS | **FAMILY** | Conveniently located on Kim Sha Beach, between the Atrium Beach Resort and the Simpson Bay Beach Resort, this bar can provide you delicious frozen drinks, a slice of pizza, burgers and fish from the grill, a beautiful sunset, and a beach bonfire on Sunday. Live music on Wednesday and Sunday and a daily happy hour from 5 to 7 makes this spot popular with both travelers and locals. Their small parking lot fills quickly; there is some on-street parking near the entrance, but parking can be a huge challenge here. ☒ *10 Billy Folly Rd., behind Festiva Atrium Beach Resort, Pelican Key* ☎ *721/523–0401* ⊕ *www.buccaneer-beachbar.com.*

Hollywood Casino

THEMED ENTERTAINMENT | Centrally located to the Simpson Bay area, the Hollywood Casino is part of Pelican Key, and is right across from Simpson Bay Resort. This casino, mostly slot machines and dice, enjoys the Hollywood Star Theme. Isola Restaurant, a very busy authentic Italian dining spot, is part of the complex. It has many traditional upscale offerings and excellent brick-oven pizzas. ☒ *37 Billy Folly Rd., Pelican Key* ☎ *721/544–4463* ⊕ *www.hollywoodcasino.info.*

Princess Casino

THEMED ENTERTAINMENT | One of the island's largest gaming halls has a wide array of restaurants and entertainment options. It's just a quick trip across the Simpson Bay Lagoon Causeway from the Simpson Bay area. ☒ *Port de Plaisance, 155 Union Rd., Cole Bay* ☎ *721/544–5222.*

Simpson Bay

 Beaches

★ Simpson Bay Beach

BEACH | This half-moon stretch of white sand on the island's Caribbean side is a hidden gem. It's mostly surrounded by private residences, with no big resorts, few Jet Skiers, and no crowds. It's just you, the sand, and the water (along with one funky beach bar, Karakter, at the beach's northern end, to provide some chairs and nourishment). The beach is sometimes a bit noisy when planes depart nearby. To find the beach, follow the signs southeast of the airport to Mary's Boon and the Horny Toad guesthouses. **Amenities:** food and drink; showers; toilets. **Best for:** solitude; swimming; walking. ☒ *Simpson Bay.*

🍴 Restaurants

★ Balls and Wine

$$ | **ECLECTIC** | **FAMILY** | This quaint restaurant with a quirky name, located in the corner of the Paradise Mall, is a hidden gem.

Owners Eduar and wife Alejandra serve appetizing tapas, delicious wine, and craft cocktails that have garnered the restaurant quite a following. **Known for:** Taco Tuesday and Wine Wednesday; friendly owners; intimate yet convivial atmosphere. [$] *Average main: $18* ⊠ *Paradise Mall, Welfare Rd., Simpson Bay* ☎ *721/527–6146* ⊕ *www.ballsandwine.com* ▬ *No credit cards* ⊘ *Closed Sun.* ☞ *Cash only.*

★ Bamboo House

$$$ | ASIAN FUSION | Located in a hilltop villa overlooking Simpson Bay, Bamboo House blends stunning views with a lively atmosphere and top-notch sushi. Chefs from spots like Nobu and Morimoto blend contemporary Asian flavors and Mediterranean traditions with complexity and innovation. **Known for:** dynamic, upbeat ambience; views at sunset; sushi and sashimi. [$] *Average main: $27* ⊠ *150 Union Rd., Simpson Bay* ☎ *721/523-1508* ⊕ *www.bamboohouse-sxm.com* ⊘ *Closed Mon.*

Beirut

$$ | LEBANESE | FAMILY | Beirut serves delicious, fresh Middle Eastern specialties such as falafel, kebabs, and salads, as well as meze such as baba ghanoush. The friendly owners make everyone feel right at home, and there's a hookah bar in the back in the evening. **Known for:** friendly staff; reasonable prices; casual, welcoming atmosphere. [$] *Average main: $18* ⊠ *29 Airport Rd., Simpson Bay* ☎ *721/545–3612* ⊕ *www.beirutsxm.com.*

★ Izi Ristorante Italiano

$$$ | ITALIAN | FAMILY | The award-winning former chef and owner of La Gondola serves up shareable portions of more than 400 dishes in this popular, cheerful, centrally located space. For something fun, diners are invited to create their own menu: pick a pasta and sauce, then add your choice of meat, fish, and veggies. **Known for:** unequaled tasting menu; homemade desserts that are worth saving room for; creative, hands-on chef. [$] *Average main: $29* ⊠ *Paradise Mall, 67 Welfare Rd., Simpson Bay* ☎ *721/544–3079* ⊕ *www.izirestaurant.com* ⊘ *Closed Mon.*

Karakter Beach Lounge

$$$ | ECLECTIC | FAMILY | This charming modern beach bar, right behind the airport, serves up fun, great music, relaxation, and a lot of style. Open from 9 am until 10 pm, with nightly live music in the evening, the restaurant makes fruit smoothies, tropical cocktails, pastas, seafood, and tapas. **Known for:** good food; on the beach; funky surroundings (an old school bus). [$] *Average main: $24* ⊠ *121 Simpson Bay Rd., Simpson Bay* ☎ *721/523–9983* ⊕ *www.karakterstmaarten.com.*

Palapa Grill

$$$ | FRENCH FUSION | French-Caribbean fusion dishes that change with the seasons keep the menu fresh at this lively restaurant in the middle of the popular Simpson Bay strip. Like the menu, each section of the restaurant is thoughtful; its varying decor creates different vibes, but still offers the intimacy of a hidden oasis. **Known for:** trendy decor; lively lounge with DJ and creative cocktails; delicious tapas. ⑤ *Average main: $28 ⊠ 28 Airport Rd., Simpson Bay ☎ 721/559–1901 ⊕ www.palapagrillsxm.com* ⊘ *Closed Sun.*

Roxxy Beach

$$$ | ASIAN FUSION | Located in the entertainment mecca of the island, Simpson Bay, this beach bar and restaurant combines the alluring vibes of St-Tropez and Miami Beach with the flavors of Asia and the Mediterranean. Live music by well-known local and international DJs make this a popular stop for many. **Known for:** beach party atmosphere; sushi and tapas; great happy hour with sunset views. ⑤ *Average main: $28 ⊠ 127 Welfare Rd., Simpson Bay ☎ 721/520–2001 ⊕ www.roxxybeach.com* ⊘ *Closed Mon.*

Rusty Rocket Rum and Burger Saloon

$$ | BURGER | FAMILY | This lively and fun spot next to the airport is famous for serving the island's best burgers. Built mostly from wooden palettes and wine boxes, the bar exudes Caribbean charm. Jimmy, the owner, has an amusing imagination, and the menu is testament to that. **Known for:** fun atmosphere, especially on the weekend; guest names written all over the bar; creative and tasty burgers. ⑤ *Average main: $15 ⊠ Across from the Winair office, 130 Airport Rd., Simpson Bay ☎ 721/556–3300 ⊕ www. facebook.com/RustyRocket* ⊘ *Closed Tues. and Wed.*

SkipJack's

$$$ | SEAFOOD | FAMILY | Arguably the island's top seafood restaurant, SkipJack's is located right on Simpson Bay lagoon. It is popular for crowd-pleasers such as its fried calamari, shrimp cocktail, sandwiches, and a good variety of fresh seafood. **Known for:** one of the biggest and busiest SXM restaurants; seasoned, friendly, knowledgeable staff; lobster from Saba. ⑤ *Average main: $21 ⊠ Welfare Rd., Simpson Bay ☎ 721/544–2313 ⊕ www. skipjacks-sxm.com.*

Vesna Taverna

$$$ | ECLECTIC | FAMILY | Centrally located just north of the Simpson Bay drawbridge, this casual restaurant is open all day long, with French and Mediterranean specials nightly and incredible house-made desserts. In the morning, you can order American breakfasts (including their famous Bagel Tower, plus omelets, pancakes, and more), and at lunch they offer tasty but healthy options like smoothies, sandwiches, salads, and burgers. **Known for:** house-made bagels; delicious house-made desserts; Greek specialties. ⑤ *Average main: $25* ✉ *9 La Palapa Marina, Simpson Bay* ✛ *In front of Soggy Dollar Bar on Simpson Bay lagoon* ☎ *721/524–5283* ⊕ *www.vesnataverna.com* ☾ *No dinner Sun. Closed Mon.*

☕ Coffee and Quick Bites

★ Top Carrot

$$ | **VEGETARIAN** | **FAMILY** | Open from 8 am to 5 pm, this friendly café and juice bar is a popular healthy breakfast and lunch stop. It features fresh and tasty vegetarian entrées, sandwiches, salads, and homemade pastries. **Known for:** casual, cozy little dining room; great gift shop; crowd-pleasing menu. ⑤ *Average main: $15* ✉ *Airport Rd., near Simpson Bay Yacht Club, Simpson Bay* ☎ *721/544–3381* ☾ *Closed Sun. and Mon. No dinner.*

★ Zee Best

$ | **CAFÉ** | This friendly bistro serves one of the most popular breakfasts on the island. There's a huge selection of fresh-baked pastries—try the almond croissants—plus sweet and savory crepes, omelets, quiches, and other treats from the oven. **Known for:** breakfast served until 2; St. Martin omelet and the zee bagel; pastry basket. ⑤ *Average main: $8* ✉ *Plaza del Lago, Simpson Bay* ☎ *721/544–2477* ⊕ *www.zeebestrestaurant.com* ▭ *No credit cards* ☾ *No dinner.*

Hotels

Azure Hotel & Art Studio

$ | **HOTEL** | **FAMILY** | Azure is a funky, wonderful boutique hotel located on a serene stretch of Simpson Bay Beach. **Pros:** central location; inexpensive; on the beach. **Cons:** no on-site restaurant (but there are kitchenettes); a car is needed to get to Philipsburg or the French side; no pool. ⑤ *Rooms from: $90* ✉ *6 Roberts Dr., Simpson Bay* ☎ *721/581–3858* ⊕ *www.azurehotelsxm.com* ⇌ *8 rooms* ⊚ *No Meals.*

★ The Horny Toad

$ | **B&B/INN** | Because of its stupendous view of Simpson Bay and the simple but comfortable rooms with creative decor, this lovely guesthouse is widely considered one of the best on this side of the island. **Pros:** tidy rooms; friendly vibe and fantastic owners;

beautiful beach that's usually deserted. **Cons:** no kids under seven; no pool (but you're on the beach); need a car to get around. ⑤ *Rooms from: $130* ✉ *2 Vlaun's Dr., Simpson Bay* ☎ *721/545–4323* ⊕ *www.thtgh.com* ⇆ *8 rooms* ⦿ *No Meals.*

Mary's Boon Beach Resort & Spa

$ | HOTEL | FAMILY | A shaded courtyard welcomes guests at this quirky, informal guesthouse on a 3-mile-long (5-km-long) stretch of Simpson Bay Beach, which has the funky feel of the Florida Keys. **Pros:** small and intimate; interesting history; owners are usually on-site. **Cons:** because of airport proximity, it can be noisy during takeoffs; basic bathrooms; very small pool. ⑤ *Rooms from: $135* ✉ *117 Simpson Bay Rd., Simpson Bay* ☎ *721/545–7000* ⊕ *www. visitmarysboon.com* ⇆ *34 rooms* ⦿ *No Meals.*

Nightlife

Buccaneer Beach Bar

BARS | FAMILY | Conveniently located on Kim Sha Beach, between the Atrium Beach Resort and the Simpson Bay Beach Resort, this bar can provide you delicious frozen drinks, a slice of pizza, burgers and fish from the grill, a beautiful sunset, and a beach bonfire on Sunday. Live music on Wednesday and Sunday and a daily happy hour from 5 to 7 makes this spot popular with both travelers and locals. Their small parking lot fills quickly; there is some on-street parking near the entrance, but parking can be a huge challenge here. ✉ *10 Billy Folly Rd., behind Festiva Atrium Beach Resort, Pelican Key* ☎ *721/523–0401* ⊕ *www.buccaneer-beachbar.com.*

Pineapple Pete

BARS | FAMILY | You can groove to nightly live music or hit the game room for a couple of rounds of pool or video games. ✉ *Airport Rd., Simpson Bay* ☎ *721/544–6030* ⊕ *www.pineapplepete.com* ⊘ *Closed Tues.*

The Red Piano

PIANO BARS | The Red Piano is one of the island's most popular entertainment venues, welcoming piano players from around the world. Famous for its "Church on Monday" event featuring a live local band, the bar has live music nightly, tasty cocktails, and a pool table. Smoking is permitted. ✉ *Across from Simpson Bay Resort, 35 Billy Folly Rd., Pelican Key* ☎ *721/527–4266.*

Little Bay

 Beaches

★ Little Bay

BEACH | Despite its occasional use by snorkelers, divers, kayakers, and boating enthusiasts, Little Bay isn't usually crowded. It does boast panoramic views of neighboring islands St. Eustatius (Statia) and Saba, and arriving and departing cruise ships. The beach is on the same peninsula as Fort Amsterdam and accessible via the Divi Little Bay Beach Resort, and most beachgoers are hotel guests. **Amenities:** food and drink at the resort; parking; toilets. **Best for:** snorkeling; swimming; walking. ⊠ *Little Bay Rd., Little Bay*.

 Hotels

★ Divi Little Bay Beach Resort

$$ | **RESORT** | **FAMILY** | Bordering gorgeous Little Bay, this centrally located property is awash with water sports, restaurants, and an awesome multilevel pool with breathtaking views of neighboring islands. **Pros:** good location; lovely beach with nearby restaurants; completely renovated. **Cons:** inconvenient entrance from the main road; car necessary to venture off-site; some construction in the area. Ⓢ *Rooms from: $275* ⊠ *Little Bay Rd., Little Bay* ☎ *721/542–2333* ⊕ *www.diviresorts.com/divi-little-bay-beach-resort* ⤵ *309 rooms*.

St. Martin (French Side)

Marigot

It is great fun to spend a few hours exploring the harbor, shopping stalls, open-air cafés, and boutiques of French St. Martin's capital, especially on Wednesday and Saturday, when the daily open-air crafts markets expand to include fresh fruits and vegetables, spices, and all manner of seafood. The market might remind you of Provence, especially when aromas of delicious cooking waft by. Be sure to climb up to the Fort St. Louis for the panoramic view, stopping at the museum for an overview of the island. Marina Port La Royale is the shopping–lunch spot central to the port, but rue de la République and rue de la Liberté, which border the bay, have some duty-free shops and boutiques. The West Indies Mall offers a deluxe (and air-conditioned) shopping experience. There's

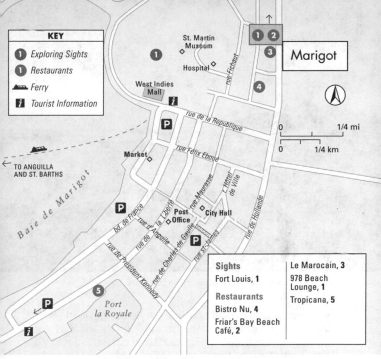

KEY

1 *Exploring Sights*
1 *Restaurants*
🚢 *Ferry*
ℹ️ *Tourist Information*

St. Martin Museum

Hospital

West Indies Mall

Marigot

rue de la République

rue Félix Eboué

← TO ANGUILLA AND ST. BARTHS

Baie de Marigot

Market

Post Office

City Hall

bd. de France

rue de la Liberté

rue d'Anguille

rue de Charles de Gaulle

rue de President Kennedy

rue St. James

rue Madresse

r. Hôtel de Ville

rue de Hollande

Port la Royale

0 ____ 1/4 mi
0 ____ 1/4 km

Sights	Le Marocain, 3
Fort Louis, 1	978 Beach Lounge, 1
Restaurants	Tropicana, 5
Bistro Nu, 4	
Friar's Bay Beach Café, 2	

less bustle here than in Philipsburg, but the open-air cafés are still tempting places to sit and people-watch. From the harborfront you can catch ferries to Anguilla and St. Barth. Parking can be a real challenge during the business day, and even at night during high season.

👁 Sights

Fort Louis

RUINS | Though not much remains of the structure itself, Fort Louis, completed by the French in 1789, is great fun if you want to climb the 92 steps to the top for the wonderful views of the island and neighboring Anguilla. On Wednesday and Saturday there is a market in the square at the bottom. ⊠ *Marigot*.

🏖 Beaches

Baie des Pères (*Friar's Bay*)

BEACH | **FAMILY** | This quiet, occasionally rocky cove close to Marigot has beach grills and bars, with chaises and umbrellas, usually calm waters, and a lovely view of Anguilla. 978 Beach Lounge, open daily for lunch and (weather permitting) dinner, has a cool jazzy vibe. It's the best place to be on the full moon,

Get the best sunset view over Marigot from Fort Louis.

with music, dancing, and a bonfire, but you can get lunch, beach chairs, and umbrellas anytime. Friar's Bay Beach Café is a French bistro on the sand, open from breakfast to sunset. To get to the beach, take National Road 7 from Marigot, go toward Grand Case to the Morne Valois hill, and turn left on the dead-end road at the sign. Note the last 200 yards of road to the beach is dirt and quite bumpy. **Amenities:** food and drink; toilets. **Best for:** partiers; swimming; walking. ⊠ *Anse des Pères.*

Happy Bay Beach (*Anse Heureuse*)
BEACH | Not many people know about this romantic, hidden gem. Happy Bay has powdery sand and stunning views of Anguilla. The snorkeling is also good. To get here, turn onto the rather rutted dead-end road to Baie des Péres (Friar's Bay). The beach itself, which is clothing-optional, is a 10- to 15-minute easy hike from the northernmost beach bar on Friar's Bay. **Amenities:** food and drink; toilets (only at adjacent Friar's Bay). **Best for:** snorkeling; solitude; swimming; walking. ⊠ *Happy Bay.*

Restaurants

Bistro Nu
$$ | FRENCH | It's hard to top the authentic French comfort food and reasonable prices you can find at this intimate restaurant tucked in a Marigot alley. Traditional French dishes like steak au poivre, sweetbreads with mushroom sauce, and sole meunière are served in a friendly, intimate dining room, which is now

St. Maarten vs. St. Martin

If this is your first trip to St. Maarten/St. Martin, you're probably wondering which side will better suit your needs. That's hard to say, because in some ways the difference between the two can seem as subtle as the open boundary dividing them. But there are some major distinctions.

St. Maarten, the Dutch side, has the casinos, more nightlife, smaller price tags (thanks in part to the French side's euro), and bigger hotels.

Cruise ships dock here. St. Martin, the French side, has no casinos, less nightlife, and hotels that are smaller and more intimate. Many have kitchenettes, and most include breakfast. If you're looking for fine dining, that used to be concentrated in Grand Case on the French side, but now there's extraordinary dining from one end of the island to the other; look especially now at both Porto Cupecoy and Simpson Bay on the Dutch side.

air-conditioned. **Known for:** good value prix-fixe menu; wine list; French comfort food. $\boxed{\$}$ *Average main: €20* ✉ *Allée de l'Ancienne Geôle, Marigot* ☎ *0690/28–16–32* ⊘ *Closed Sat. and Sun.*

★ Friar's Bay Beach Café

$$ | **BISTRO** | **FAMILY** | There is a sophisticated vibe at this quiet, rather elegant beach club that may make you feel as if you're on a private beach. You can rent lounge chairs and umbrellas (half price with lunch) and spend the whole day relaxing, drinking, and dining. **Known for:** informal atmosphere; good specials; beachside dining. $\boxed{\$}$ *Average main: €18* ✉ *Friar's Bay Rd., Anse des Pères* ☎ *0690/49–16–87* ▭ *No credit cards* ⊘ *No dinner. Closed Tues.*

★ Le Marocain

$$ | **MOROCCAN** | Years after being destroyed by Hurricane Irma, the old Marrakech is back with the same ownership but a new name, Le Marocain. The decor transports you straight to Morocco as you dine on fragrant, authentic Moroccan classics in a romantic space with an open garden and a new rooftop. **Known for:** tagine and couscous; rooftop lounge; affable staff. $\boxed{\$}$ *Average main: €20* ✉ *169 rue de Hollande, Marigot* ☎ *0590/27–54–48* ⊕ *www.le-ma-rocain.com* ⊘ *Closed Sun. No lunch.*

978 Beach Lounge

$$ | **CREOLE** | **FAMILY** | Feel the St. Martin culture at this beach bar and restaurant (previously Kali's, but now under new ownership). Flavorful local Creole dishes and island-inspired cocktails are served on the beach. **Known for:** all-white full moon beach party;

A Tale of Two Islands

The smallest island in the world to be shared between two different countries, St. Maarten/St. Martin has existed peacefully in its divided state for more than 370 years. The Treaty of Concordia, which subdivided the island, was signed in 1648 and was really inspired by the two resident colonies of French and Dutch settlers (not to mention their respective governments) joining forces to repel a common enemy, the Spanish, in 1644. Although the French were promised the side of the island facing Anguilla and the Dutch the south side of the island, the boundary itself wasn't firmly established until 1817 and only then after several disputes (16 of them, to be exact).

Visitors to the island will likely not be able to tell that they have passed from the Dutch to the French side unless they notice the border monuments at the side of the roads—and that roads on the French side feel a little smoother. In 2003 the population of St. Martin (and St. Barthélemy) voted to secede from Guadeloupe, the administrative capital of the French West Indies. That detachment became official in 2007, and St. Martin is now officially known as the Collectivité de Saint-Martin.

live music on weekends; Creole and Cajun delicacies. $ *Average main: €20* ⊠ *Friar's Bay, 61 rue de Friar's Bay, Anse des Pères* ☎ *0590/690–828–000* ⊕ *www.978sxm.com* ☺ *Closed Mon. and Tues.*

Tropicana

$$$ | **FRENCH** | This bustling and popular bistro at the Marina Port La Royale stays busy thanks to a varied menu, (relatively) reasonable prices, and friendly staff. Salads are superb lunch options, especially the salade Niçoise with medallions of crusted goat cheese. **Known for:** steak and seafood; crème brûlée; inside and outside dining. $ *Average main: €22* ⊠ *Marina Port La Royale, Marigot* ☎ *0590/87–79–07.*

Shopping

Max Mara

MIXED CLOTHING | These beautifully made, tailored clothes have an elegant attitude. ⊠ *33 rue du Kennedy, Marigot* ☎ *0590/52–99–75* ☺ *Closed Sun.*

Minguet Art Gallery

ART GALLERIES | On Rambaud Hill between Marigot and Grand Case, this gallery is managed by the daughter of the late artist Alexandre Minguet. It carries original paintings, lithographs, posters, and postcards depicting island flora and landscapes by Minguet and is a popular tourist attraction on the island. Call before visiting to be sure they're open. ⊠ *Rambaud Hill, Rambaud* ⊕ *www.minguet.com*.

French Cul de Sac

North of Orient Bay Beach, the French colonial mansion of St. Martin's mayor is nestled in the hills. Little red-roof houses look like open umbrellas tumbling down the green hillside. The area is peaceful and good for hiking. From the beach here, shuttle boats make the five-minute trip to Îlet Pinel, an uninhabited island that's fine for picnicking, snorkeling, sunning, and swimming. There are full-service restaurants and beach clubs there, so just pack the sunscreen and head over.

 Beaches

★ Îlet Pinel

BEACH | **FAMILY** | A protected nature reserve, this kid-friendly island is a five-minute ferry ride from French Cul de Sac (about €12 per person round-trip). The ferry runs every half hour from midmorning until 4 pm. The water is clear and shallow, and the shore is sheltered. Snorkelers can swim a trail between both coasts of this pencil-shape speck in the ocean. You can rent equipment on the island. There are two restaurants, Karibuni and Yellow Beach; both offer great service, with cocktail tables in the water. Chairs and umbrellas can be rented for about €25 for two. It can get busy on Sunday. **Amenities:** food and drink; parking. **Best for:** snorkeling; sunning; swimming. ⊠ *Ilet Pinel*.

 Hotels

Karibuni Boutique Hotel

$$ | **HOTEL** | Tucked away in a tropical oasis overlooking turquoise water and distant islets like Îlet Pinel and Tintamarre, this family-owned and -operated boutique hotel offers well-designed rooms in an idyllic setting. **Pros:** complimentary kayaks, transportation to Pinel island, and beach chairs; private, intimate, and peaceful; personalized service. **Cons:** no kids under 13; not on the beach (but you have a plunge pool); location is far from main areas so

Anse Marcel Beach is a great spot for swimming, dining, and lounging.

you'll need a car to get around. ⑤ *Rooms from: €350* ✉ *Cul de Sac Bay, Cul de Sac* ☎ *0590/690–64–38–58* ⊕ *www.lekaribuni.com* ☉ *Closed Sept. to mid Oct.* ⦿ *Free Breakfast.*

Anse Marcel

Restaurants

★ Anse Marcel Beach
$$$ | MODERN FRENCH | Beachside calm with a side order of chic is on the menu at this lovely and private cove restaurant/beach club that was designed with the environment in mind. It's good for a beach day, a sunset cocktail, and great swimming. **Known for:** modern, pleasant atmosphere; beachfront dining; seafood, especially the local catch. ⑤ *Average main: €24* ✉ *Anse Marcel Beach, Anse Marcel* ☎ *0690/26–38–50* ⊕ *www.ansemarcelbeach.com.*

🛏 Hotels

Anse Marcel Beach Resort
$ | RESORT | FAMILY | This classic property on 148 acres of lush gardens borders the exceptionally beautiful and secluded beach in Anse Marcel. **Pros:** all-inclusive option; lovely gardens; beachfront setting. **Cons:** need a car to get around; beach is shared; some rooms have round bathtubs in middle of room. ⑤ *Rooms*

from: $147 ⊠ *26 rue de Lonvillier, Anse Marcel* ☎ *0590/26–38–50* ⊗ *Closed Sept.–Oct.* ➪ *129 rooms* ❖ *No Meals.*

Secrets St. Martin Resort and Spa
$ | RESORT | Reopened in 2021, this all-inclusive hotel has 300 rooms from partial ocean view to swim-out suites, plus multiple dining options, including Asian, Italian, French restaurants, a café, and a poolside grill. **Pros:** secluded and intimate; activities galore; great beach and huge pool. **Cons:** beach may be busy; a car is necessary to explore outside of resort; remote. Ⓢ *Rooms from: €269* ⊠ *BP 581, Anse Marcel* ☎ *0590/87–67–00* ⊕ *www.secretsresorts. com* ➪ *300 rooms* ❖ *All-Inclusive.*

Sol e Luna Guesthouse
$$ | B&B/INN | Independent couples who don't want a big resort love the six comfortable suites in this hillside guesthouse overlooking a pretty pool, a salt pond, and on to Orient Bay. Beautifully decorated in a modern Italian style with tropical details, the attractive and spacious suites have Italian marble baths, compact kitchenettes, and dining patios. **Pros:** spacious suites; good location for exploring; excellent on-site restaurant. **Cons:** need a car; quite a few steps to climb around the property; not a full-service hotel. Ⓢ *Rooms from: €280* ⊠ *61 Mont Vernon, Baie Orientale* ☎ *0590/29–08–56* ⊗ *Closed Sept.* ➪ *6 suites* ❖ *Free Breakfast.*

Baie Nettlé

Beaches

Baie Rouge
BEACH | Here you can bask with millionaires renting big-ticket villas in the "neighborhood" of Terres Basses—the French lowlands. The gorgeous beach and its salt ponds make up a nature preserve, site of the oldest habitation in the Caribbean. This area is widely thought to have the best snorkeling on the island. You can swim the crystal waters along the point and explore a swim-through cave, but beware: the water can be rough. There is a sign and a right turn after you leave Baie Nettlé. **Amenities:** none. **Best for:** snorkeling; swimming; walking. ⊠ *Baie Rouge.*

🍴 Restaurants

★ La Cigale
$$$$ | FRENCH | On the edge of Baie Nettlé, this restaurant has wonderful views of the lagoon from its dining room and open-air patio, but the charm comes from the devoted attention of

adorable owner Olivier, helped by his mother and brother and various cousins. The delicious food is edible sculpture: lobster bisque under a pastry dome, fresh sea bass with a leek fondue, and their signature "Le Cigale," a foie gras emulsion soup. **Known for:** excellent service; convenient location near Marigot; artistic presentation. ⑤ *Average main: €32* ⊠ *101 Laguna Beach, Baie Nettlé* ☎ *0590/87–90–23* ⊕ *www.lacigalerestaurantsxm.com* ⊗ *Closed Sun. and Sept. and Oct. No lunch.*

Mezza Luna

$$$ | **ITALIAN** | **FAMILY** | Sit with your feet in the sand and enjoy the views at this restaurant, popular for its pizzas and beach terrace. Their chalkboard describes all the varieties, which are many, and the pricing is very reasonable. **Known for:** house-made pasta; reasonable prices; variety of pizza. ⑤ *Average main: €22* ⊠ *501 Nettlé Bay Beach Club, Baie Nettlé* ☎ *0590/690–73–19–18* ⊕ *www. facebook.com/mezzalunasxm* ⊗ *Closed Sun.*

Grand Case

"The Culinary Capital of the Caribbean" is back. Years after rebuilding from big damages sustained during Hurricane Irma, Grand Case's popular eateries on its renowned "Restaurant Row" are once again serving exquisite dishes. It's an easy 10-minute drive from either Orient Bay or Marigot, stretching along a narrow beach overlooking Anguilla. At lunchtime, or with kids, head to the casual *lolos* (open-air grills) and feet-in-the-sand beach bars. At night, stroll the strip and preview the sophisticated offerings on the menus posted outside before you settle in for a long and sumptuous meal (reservations are required for some of the top restaurants, and they're essential in winter, high season).

Beaches

Baie de Grand Case

BEACH | **FAMILY** | Along this skinny stripe of a beach bordering the culinary village of Grand Case, the old-style gingerbread architecture sometimes peeps out between the bustling restaurants and boutiques. The sea is usually quite calm, and there are tons of fun lunch options from bistros to beachside grills (called *lolos*). Several of the restaurants rent chairs and umbrellas; some include their use for lunch patrons. The main street, nicknamed "Restaurant Row" is where some of the best restaurants on the island can be found. In between there is a bit of shopping—for beach necessities but also for handicrafts and beach couture. **Amenities:** food and drink; toilets. **Best for:** swimming; walking. ⊠ *Grand Case.*

🍴 Restaurants

★ Bacchus

$$$ | FRENCH | The best wine importer in the Caribbean, Benjamin Laurent, and his wife Magali have built a lively, immaculate, deliciously air-conditioned wine cellar that also happens to serve outstanding starters, salads, and main courses made from top ingredients brought in from France. The place is well worth the effort it may take to find it, in the Hope Estate commercial area south of the main road (Deviation de Grand Case). **Known for:** chic bistro setting; strong coffee; great wine. ⑤ *Average main: €28* ⊠ *18–19 Hope Estate, Grand Case Rd., Grand Case* ☏ *0590/87–15–70* ⊕ *www.bacchussxm.com* ⊗ *Closed Sun. No dinner.*

★ Cynthia's Talk of the Town

$$ | CARIBBEAN | FAMILY | One of the five lolos in the middle of the village on the water side, Cynthia's (better known simply as "Talk of the Town") is a fun, relatively cheap, and iconic St. Martin meal. With plastic utensils and paper plates, it couldn't be more informal, and the menu includes everything from succulent grilled ribs to stewed conch, fresh snapper, and grilled lobster. **Known for:** succulent ribs; low pricing and big portions; lobster. ⑤ *Average main: €14* ⊠ *Bd. de Grand Case, Grand Case* ▭ *No credit cards.*

L'Auberge Gourmande

$$$ | FRENCH | With a formal, French-provincial room framed by elegant arches, L'Auberge Gourmande is in one of the island's oldest Creole houses. On the walls are small etchings that look like they're 100 years old, but they're actually contemporary works by renowned island impressionist Sir Roland Richardson. **Known for:** Dover sole in almond butter; creative desserts; high-end traditional dining. ⑤ *Average main: €27* ⊠ *89 bd. de Grand Case, Grand Case* ☏ *0590/87–73–37* ⊕ *www.laubergegourmande.com* ⊗ *Closed Sept. No lunch.*

La Villa

$$$ | FRENCH | FAMILY | Diners flock here for the friendly management, the spectrum of well-prepared French cuisine, and the easy-to-find location in the middle of Grand Case. You can choose what you like from their €52 three-course menu (additional charges for foie gras and lobster), or go à la carte. **Known for:** friendly service; three-course fixed-price menu; classic seafood preparations. ⑤ *Average main: €28* ⊠ *93 bd. de Grand Case, Grand Case*

☎ *0590/690–501–204* ⊕ *www.lavillasxm.com* ◷ *No lunch. Closed Wed.*

Le Cottage

$$$ | **FRENCH** | French cuisine with Caribbean flavors is prepared with a light touch and presented with flair at Le Cottage, where a lively community gathers on the street-front porch. With an amazing wine cellar and a sommelier from the Burgundy region, the restaurant offers a great wine-pairing menu at €89. **Known for:** wine-pairing menu; coveted porch seating that should be reserved in advance; loyal following. ⑤ *Average main: €30* ✉ *97 bd. de Grand Case, Grand Case* ☎ *0590/690–622–686* ⊕ *www.lecottagesxm.com* ◷ *No lunch.*

★ Rainbow Café & Beach Bar

$$$ | **MODERN FRENCH** | With a highly Instagrammable Bohemian look, this restaurant brings style, wit, and a bit of panache to the beach bar genre. Rainbow delivers a memorable breakfast, lunch, sunset drinks, sushi, and tapas—on the beach, their beachfront deck, or on the covered rooftop. **Known for:** beach parties; people-watching; SXM's most upscale beach bar. ⑤ *Average main: €30* ✉ *176 bd. de Grand Case, Grand Case* ☎ *590/690–888–444* ⊕ *www.rainbowcafesxm.com* ◷ *Closed Sept.*

Spiga

$$$ | **ITALIAN** | In a beautifully restored Creole house, exceptional cuisine fuses Italian and occasionally some Caribbean ingredients and cooking techniques. Follow one of the ample appetizers with an excellent pasta, fresh fish, or meat dish, such as the braised Angus beef short rib with porcini mushroom risotto. **Known for:** porch dining; outstanding desserts; creative Italian cuisine. ⑤ *Average main: €26* ✉ *4 rte. de L'Espérance, Grand Case* ☎ *0590/52–47–83* ⊕ *www.spiga-sxm.com* ◷ *Closed mid-Sept.–late Oct. and Tues. No lunch.*

Hotels

Bleu Emeraude

$$$ | **APARTMENT** | **FAMILY** | Be lulled to sleep by the sounds of the ocean below at one of the 11 spacious apartments in this tidy complex that sits right on a sliver of Grand Case Beach. **Pros:** modern and updated; walk to restaurants; attractive decor. **Cons:** far from Philipsburg, the island's shopping capital; can be an hour or more from the airport on busy days; neighborhood can be noisy. ⑤ *Rooms from: €390* ✉ *240 bd. de Grand Case, Grand Case* ☎ *0590/690-71–12–16, 0590/690–37–07–00* ⊕ *www.bleuemeraude.com* ⇨ *11 units* ⦾ *Free Breakfast.*

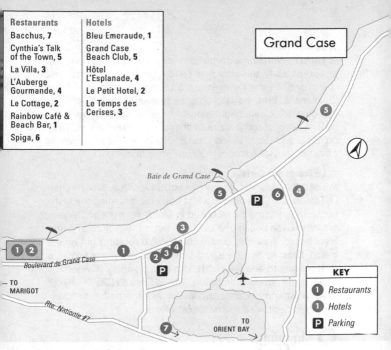

Restaurants	Hotels
Bacchus, **7**	Bleu Emeraude, **1**
Cynthia's Talk of the Town, **5**	Grand Case Beach Club, **5**
La Villa, **3**	Hôtel L'Esplanade, **4**
L'Auberge Gourmande, **4**	Le Petit Hotel, **2**
Le Cottage, **2**	Le Temps des Cerises, **3**
Rainbow Café & Beach Bar, **1**	
Spiga, **6**	

Grand Case

Baie de Grand Case

Boulevard de Grand Case

TO MARIGOT

Rte. Nationale #7

TO ORIENT BAY

KEY
1 Restaurants
1 Hotels
P Parking

Grand Case Beach Club

$$ | RESORT | FAMILY | Easily the finest beach resort in Grand Case, "GCBC" has a friendly staff and incredible sunset views. **Pros:** reasonably priced for what you get; access to two beaches; Grand Case beach and La Petite Plage; walking distance to fine-dining restaurants. **Cons:** some ongoing minor renovations; need a car to explore; narrow road to hotel gets congested on Sunday. $ *Rooms from: €326 ⊠ 21 rue de la Petite Plage, at East / North end of bd. de Grand Case, Grand Case* ☎ *0590/87–51–87, 800/344–3016 in U.S.* ⊕ *www.grandcasebeachclub.com* ⇨ *72 apartments* ᴼ *No Meals.*

★ Hôtel L'Esplanade

$$$ | HOTEL | FAMILY | Fans return year after year to the classy, loft-style suites in this immaculate family-owned and-operated boutique hotel, located on a hill overlooking Grand Case village and its harbor. **Pros:** highly attentive management; clean and beautiful; family-friendly. **Cons:** lots of stairs; not on the beach; the pool, spa, and yoga area are a bit of a walk from the rooms. $ *Rooms from: €415 ⊠ Grand Case* ☎ *0590/87–06–55, 866/596–8365 in U.S.* ⊕ *www.lesplanade.com* ⇨ *24 units* ᴼ *Free Breakfast.*

★ Le Petit Hotel

$$ | HOTEL | With some of the best restaurants in the Caribbean just steps away, this attractive beachfront boutique hotel exudes charm and has the same caring, attentive management as Hotel L'Esplanade. **Pros:** walking distance to everything in Grand Case; friendly staff; clean, bright, updated rooms. **Cons:** no pool; on-site parking is tight; some stairs to climb. $ *Rooms from: €275* ⊠ *248 bd. de Grand Case, Grand Case* ☎ *0590/29–09–65* ⊕ *www.lepetithotel.com* ⇌ *10 rooms* ❖| *Free Breakfast.*

★ Le Temps des Cerises

$$ | B&B/INN | Named for the classic 19th-century French chanson, Le Temps des Cerises is the first hotel representing the fashion house of the same name based in Marseille; right on the sands of Grand Case beach, the boutique inn is the picture of current French chic. **Pros:** chic decor; comfortable rooms; right on the beach. **Cons:** across the island from Princess Juliana airport; a car is necessary to see the sights; can be a bit noisy. $ *Rooms from: €290* ⊠ *158 bd. de Grand Case, Grand Case* ☎ *590/51–36–27* ⊕ *www.letempsdescerises.com/en/saint-martin-beach-hotel* ❖ *Closed Sept.* ⇌ *8 rooms* ❖| *No Meals.*

🛍 Shopping

Tropismes Gallery

ART GALLERIES | Contemporary Caribbean artists showcased here include Paul Elliot Thuleau, who is a master of capturing the sunshine of the islands, and Nathalie Lepine, whose portraits show a Modigliani influence. This is a serious gallery with some very good artists. It's open 10–1 and 5–9 daily. ⊠ *107 bd. de Grand Case, Grand Case* ☎ *690/54–62–69* ⊕ *www.tropismesgallery.com* ❖ *Closed Sun.*

Voila!!!

MIXED CLOTHING | The trendy beach attire, artsy accessories, and souvenirs are fun to try on and buy here. They're open until 9 pm, which means you can shop here before dinner. ⊠ *101 bd. de Grand Case, Grand Case* ☎ *0590/690–37–72–41* ❖ *Closed Sun. morning.*

Orléans

North of Oyster Pond and the Étang aux Poissons (Fish Lake) is the island's oldest settlement, also known as the French Quarter. You can still see a few vibrantly painted West Indian–style homes with the original gingerbread fretwork. There are also large areas of the nature and marine preserve working to save the island's fragile ecosystem.

 Beaches

Le Gallon

BEACH | FAMILY | A coral reef borders this quiet, naturally well-protected beach, part of the French side's nature reserve. The water is calm, clear, and quite shallow, so it's a paradise for young kids. Kiteboarders and windsurfers like the trade winds at the far end of the beach and will find the beach satisfactory if they don't need those "services." On Sunday there still may be some groups picnicking and partying, but during the week Le Galion is a rather desolate place better avoided. **Amenities:** parking. **Best for:** small children; swimming; windsurfing. ⊠ *Quartier d'Orléans.*

 Restaurants

Yvette's Restaurant

$$ | CARIBBEAN | FAMILY | Follow the locals to Yvette's Kitchen, in a private house, for the island's best creole-Cajun cooking. All the St. Martin favorites are dished up in big portions at a reasonable price. **Known for:** hot johnnycakes; curry goat; pickled conch. ⑤ *Average main: €19* ⊠ *Quartier d'Orléans* ✛ *Off the main road of Quartier d'Orleans, across the road from the pharmacy* ☎ *721/524–6946* ▭ *No credit cards* ⊗ *Closed Wed.*

Pic Paradis

Between Marigot and Grand Case, Paradise Peak (Pic Paradis), at 1,492 feet, is the island's highest point. There are two observation areas. From them, the tropical forest unfolds below, and the vistas are breathtaking. The road is quite isolated and steep, best suited to a four-wheel-drive vehicle. There continue to be some problems with crime in this area, so it might be best to go hiking with an experienced local guide, if at all; better to visit Loterie Farm, which is off the main road headed to Pic Paradis.

◉ Sights

★ Loterie Farm

NATURE PRESERVE | FAMILY | Almost halfway up the road to Pic Paradis is a peaceful 150-acre private nature preserve, opened to the public in 1999 by American expat B. J. Welch. There are trail maps, so you can hike on your own or hire a guide. Marked trails

Whether you're on St. Maarten or St. Martin, the sunsets are unforgettable.

traverse native forest with tamarind, gum, mango, and mahogany trees—the same as it was hundreds of years ago. You might well see some wild vervet monkeys, now rather common here. The Jungle Pool is a lovely tropical garden with a large pool and Jacuzzi area plus lounge chairs, great music, roaming iguanas, and chic tented cabanas with a St. Barth–meets–Wet 'n' Wild atmosphere. A delicious, healthy lunch or dinner can be had poolside, and if you are brave—and over 4 feet 5 inches tall—you can try soaring over trees on one of the longest ziplines in the western hemisphere. (There is a milder version, but people love the more extreme one.) On Sundays you can enjoy music, played by a dj in the tree booth. Called "TreeJ" this wild party by the pool is from 1pm to 5pm on Sundays, and is has more of an adults vibe. If the festive pool area is not your thing, head to the Jungle Room for a tasty lunch, great ambience, tapas, and strong cocktails. ⊠ *103 rte. de Pic du Paradis, Rambaud* ☎ *0590/87–86–16* ⊕ *www.loteriefarm.com* 🚹 *Hiking €10, zipline €40–€60, cabanas from €85, and day beds at €25* ⚓ *Cabana reservation recommended.*

Baie Orientale

 Beaches

★ Baie Orientale (*Orient Bay*)
BEACH | FAMILY | The beach is as vibrant as ever (wider even, with more sand to enjoy now than in years past). Many consider this

the island's most beautiful beach, with 2 miles (3 km) of champagne sand, underwater marine reserve, a variety of water sports, and trendy beach clubs. At its southern end, "naturists" enjoy the Club Orient area's clothing-optional policy, limited by regulation to that portion of the beach only. (Topless sunbathing is allowed on the entire beach.) Naturally, cameras are forbidden and may be confiscated. Plan to spend the day at one of the clubs; each bar has different color umbrellas, and most boast excellent restaurants and lively entertainment. To get here from Marigot, take the main road north past Grand Case, past the French side Aéroport de L'Espérance, and watch for the left turn. **Amenities:** food and drink; parking; toilets; water sports. **Best for:** nudists; partiers; swimming; walking; windsurfing. ⊠ Baie Orientale.

🍴 Restaurants

Coco Beach
$$$ | FRENCH FUSION | This trendy beach restaurant captivates guests with its chic decor and relaxing vibes. Enjoy beach service or hang by the bar for flavorful cocktails. **Known for:** beachfront relaxation; tartare, lobster, and oysters; Sunday entertainment. $ Average main: €30 ⊠ Orient Bay Beach, Baie Orientale ☎ 0590/690–64–14–94 ⊕ www.cocobeach.restaurant ⊗ No dinner, closed Sept.

★ L'Astrolabe
$$$ | FRENCH | L'Astrolabe gets raves for its modern interpretations of classic French cuisine served around the pool at this cozy, relaxed restaurant in the Esmeralda Resort. Menu highlights include lobster and cognac bisque, fresh sea scallops and smoked pork belly, foie gras over brioche, Angus beef filet mignon, and fresh vanilla crème brûlée. **Known for:** fixed-price lobster menu on Friday; live music on Monday and Friday; classic French dining, by the pool. $ Average main: €28 ⊠ Esmeralda Resort, Baie Orientale ☎ 0590/87–11–20 ⊕ www.astrolabe-sxm.com ⊗ No lunch. No dinner Wed.

L'Atelier
$$$$ | FRENCH FUSION | Located on the square in Orient Bay village, this popular French restaurant enthralls with flavors for every palate. Owner Alexandre's food is inspired by his grandmother; tasteful dishes made with simple, fresh ingredients have become a staple. **Known for:** steaks and bone marrow appetizers; exciting menu presented on a blackboard; cocktails by expert mixologists. $ Average main: €35 ⊠ Orient Bay village square, Baie Orientale ☎ 0590/690–22–10–22 ⊗ Closed Sun. and Aug.

Hotels

Esmeralda Resort

$ | **RESORT** | **FAMILY** | Esmeralda has traditional Caribbean-style, kitchen-equipped villas that can be configured to meet guests' needs, have their own pool, and offer the fun of Orient Beach a short walk away. **Pros:** beachfront location; private pools; plenty of activities. **Cons:** iffy Wi-Fi service; main airport and capital is a distance away, especially with traffic; need a car to get around. ⑤ *Rooms from: €262* ⊠ *Baie Orientale, 44 Main St., Baie Orientale* ☎ *0590/87–36–36* ⊕ *www.esmeralda-resort.com* ۞ *Closed Sept.* ➾ *65 rooms* ⵏ◎ⵏ *Free Breakfast.*

★ Hotel La Plantation

$$ | **HOTEL** | **FAMILY** | This quaint, colonial-style hotel is a charmer; French doors open to a wraparound verandah with an expansive view of the bay. **Pros:** relaxing atmosphere; seating privileges at nearby restaurants; lots of area restaurants. **Cons:** beach is a 10-minute walk away; car or taxi needed to get to other major tourist areas; small pool. ⑤ *Rooms from: €283* ⊠ *C5 Parc de La Baie Orientale, Baie Orientale* ☎ *800/480-8555 toll free, 0590/29–58–00* ⊕ *www.laplantationhotel.com* ۞ *Normally closed Sept.– mid-Oct.* ➾ *51 rooms* ⵏ◎ⵏ *Free Breakfast.*

★ La Playa Orient Bay

$$ | **RESORT** | You can't miss the multistory white villas right on beautiful Orient Beach, beautifully renovated after Hurricane Irma; guests flock here for reasonable though not cheap prices, huge rooms, and the friendly, relaxed atmosphere. **Pros:** spacious rooms; friendly atmosphere; attractive beach location. **Cons:** car needed to visit other tourist areas; getting to the airport can take up to an hour on weekdays (traffic); minimum length stay may be required in high season. ⑤ *Rooms from: $296* ⊠ *116 Parc de la Baie Orientale, Baie Orientale* ☎ *0590/87–42–08* ⊕ *www.laplayaorientbay.com* ➾ *56 rooms* ⵏ◎ⵏ *Free Breakfast.*

★ Palm Court at Orient Beach Hotel

$ | **HOTEL** | **FAMILY** | The romantic beachfront units of this *hôtel de charme* are steps from the fun of Orient Beach yet private, quiet, and stylish. **Pros:** big rooms; romantic decor; nice garden. **Cons:** car required to get to distant key tourist areas; daily except Sunday, driving in traffic to the airport can take an hour; across from, but not on, the beach. ⑤ *Rooms from: €231* ⊠ *Parc de la Baie Orientale, Baie Orientale* ☎ *800/480–8555, 0590/87–41–94* ⊕ *www.sxm-palm-court.com* ۞ *Closed Oct.* ➾ *21 rooms* ⵏ◎ⵏ *Free Breakfast.*

Belmond La Samanna is known for its great beach and spa.

Shopping

Antoine Chapon

ART GALLERIES | Reflecting the peaceful atmosphere of St. Martin and the sea surrounding it, the watercolor paintings of Antoine Chapon can be seen at the artist's studio in Cul de Sac. Call for an appointment. ✉ *Terrasses de Cul de Sac, Cul de Sac* ☎ *0590/87–40–87* ⊕ *www.chaponartgallery.com.*

Baie Longue

Beaches

Baie Longue (*Long Bay*)

BEACH | Though it extends over the French Lowlands, from the cliff at La Samanna to La Pointe des Canniers, the island's longest beach has no facilities or vendors. It's a great place for a romantic walk, but be aware that getting here isn't as easy as it once was since you must now pass through Lowlands security. Note that the beach faces westward and can get very hot; there's no shade from trees, either. This beach is on the leeward, less breezy side of the island. To get here, take National Road 7 south of Marigot. Baie Longue Road is the first entrance to the beach. It's worth a splurge for lunch or a sunset cocktail at the elegant La Samanna. **Amenities:** none. **Best for:** solitude; walking. Note: beach faces westward and can get very hot; there's no shade from trees, either. This beach is on the leeward, less breezy side of the island. ⊠ *Baie Longue.*

Hotels

★ Belmond La Samanna

$$$$ | **RESORT** | **FAMILY** | A complete redesign of the rooms, villas, and restaurants in 2019 has helped keep La Samanna, bordered by a pristine, white-sand beach, the island's top luxury resort. **Pros:** chic decor; great beach and spa; beach cabanas, convenient location. **Cons:** some rooms are small for the price; car required to get to off-site restaurants and shopping; expensive. ⑤ *Rooms from: €1071* ⊠ *Baie Longue* ☎ *0590/87–64–00, 800/854–2252 in U.S.* ⊕ *www.belmond.com/lasamanna* ⊗ *Usually closed Sept. and Oct.* ⇌ *91 rooms* ⭕ *No Meals.*

Activities

Biking and Scooters

Biking is a great way to explore the island. Beginner and intermediate cyclists can ride the coastal roads from Cay Bay to Fort Amsterdam or Mullet Beach. More serious bikers can cruise from Bellevue Trail and Port de Plaisance to Marigot. Bring your bathing suit—along the way you can stop at Baie Rouge or Baie des Prunes for a dip. Biking to Fort Louis offer fabulous views. The most challenging ride is up Pic Paradis. You should only tackle this route with a guide, because of crime here; ask at one of the bike shops. Several locally known guides can help you make this trip. There are no bike lanes and many roads are narrow, so pedal with caution and be aware of nearby traffic.

TriSport

BIKING | **FAMILY** | Rental bikes here come with helmets, water bottles, locks, and repair kits. Rates are $20 per day, $25 overnight, and $110 per week. A variety of guided bicycle tours focusing on hard terrain, or historical insight are offered for $49–$75. TriSport also rents kayaks and stand-up paddleboards, and arranges hikes, outings, and even triathlons. ■ **TIP→ If you are on the French side, there is a location in Marigot.** ⊠ *14B Airport Rd., Simpson Bay* ☎ *721/545–4384* ⊕ *www.trisportsxm.com.*

Boating and Sailing

The water and winds are perfect for skimming the surf. It'll cost you anywhere between $700 and $3,000 per day to rent a powerboat, considerably less if you join one of the many sailing tours available. Drinks and lunch are usually included on crewed day charters, and some tours are eco-oriented.

★ Pyratz Gourmet Sailing

SAILING | FAMILY | This company offers the ultimate sailing experience on their power catamaran, complete with a gourmet four-course lunch, wine, cocktails, and activities such as a floating mat, kayaking, paddle boarding, and snorkeling. Everything from the water toys to the reef-safe sunscreen is provided, making it easy to relax and enjoy a full day on the water. Or, you can watch the sun go down on their sunset cruise in a group of eight on the *Bali 4.5* or on the *Lagoon 450 S* power catamaran. Rent both vessels for larger groups. The company prides itself on its sustainability efforts and environmentally friendly practices. ✉ *50 Airport Rd., Simpson Bay* ☎ *0590/690–88–81–11* ⊕ *www.pyratzsxm.com* ☞ *Shared charters on Tues.*

Random Wind

BOATING | FAMILY | This company offers full-day sailing and snorkeling trips on a catamaran, also called *Random Wind*. Charter prices depend on the size of the group and whether lunch is served. The regularly scheduled Paradise Daysail (10–3, $119 per person for adults, $95 kids 5–12) includes food and drink, snorkeling equipment, and stand-up paddleboard. Departures, weekdays at 9:45, are from the cruise ship terminal in Philipsburg or from Simpson Bay, by prearrangement. Everyone loves "flying" from the Tarzan swing. ■ TIP→ **You can get the best rates from the website rather than hotels or cruise lines.** ✉ *Simpson Bay* ☎ *757/660–5624, 721/587–5742* ⊕ *www.randomwind.com.*

Rhino Safari

BOATING | FAMILY | Take a 2½-hour guided water tour around the island on a 10-foot inflatable watercraft. The boats are stable, easy to pilot, and riding the waves is a blast. The tour includes 45 minutes of snorkeling (equipment provided) at Creole Rock, the best snorkeling spot on the island. Choose from several departures and routes every day. There is a $6 marina park fee to be paid at check-in. ✉ *58 Welfare Rd., Simpson Bay* ☎ *721/544–3150* ⊕ *www.rhinotours.com* ✒ *From $75 per person.*

St. Maarten 12-Metre Challenge

BOATING | Sailing experience is not necessary as participants compete on 68-foot racing yachts, including Dennis Connor's *Stars and Stripes* (the actual boat that won the America's Cup in Freemantle, Australia, in 1987), *Canada II,* and *True North I.* Everyone is allocated a crew position, either grinding winches, trimming sails, punching the stopwatch, or bartending. The thrill is priceless, but book well in advance; this is one of the most popular shore excursions in the Caribbean. It is offered up to four times daily and lasts 2½–3 hours. Children over 12 (9 with sailing experience) may participate. ⊠ *Bobby's Marina, Philipsburg* ☎ *721/542–0045* ⊕ *www.12metre.com.*

Diving

Diving in St. Maarten/St. Martin has become a major attraction, with reef expeditions and sunken boats easily accessible offshore. The seawater temperature here is rarely below 78°F and visibility is often 60 to 100 feet. The island has more than 30 dive sites, from wrecks to rocky labyrinths. Right outside Philipsburg, 55 feet under the water, is the HMS *Proselyte,* once explored by Jacques Cousteau. Although it sank in 1801, the boat's cannons and coral-encrusted anchors are still visible.

Off the northwest coast, in the protected and mostly current-free Grand Case Bay, is **Creole Rock.** The water here ranges in depth from 10 feet to 25 feet. Other sites off the northern coast include **Î let Pinel,** with shallow diving; **Green Key,** with its vibrant barrier reef; and **Tintamarre,** with its sheltered coves and geologic faults. On average, one-tank dives start at $65; two-tank dives are about $115. Certification courses start at about $450.

The Dutch side offers several full-service outfitters and SSI (Scuba Schools International) and/or PADI certification. There are no hyperbaric chambers on the island.

Dive Safaris

SCUBA DIVING | Certified divers who have dived within the last two years can watch professional feeders give reef sharks a little nosh in a half-hour shark-awareness dive. The company also offers a full PADI training program and can tailor dive excursions and sophisticated, sensitive instruction to any level. ⊠ *16 Airport Rd., Simpson Bay* ☎ *721/520–3618* ⊕ *www.divesafarisstmaarten.com.*

Ocean Explorers Dive Center

SCUBA DIVING | St. Maarten's oldest dive shop offers different types of certification courses. Serious divers like the eight-person-maximum policy on trips, but this means you must reserve in advance. Have a small group? You can easily reserve the entire boat, given sufficient notice. Learn to dive with their on-site PADI courses or get started from home with their PADI e-Learning. ⊠ 113 Welfare Rd., Simpson Bay ☎ 721/544–5252 ⊕ www.stmaartendiving.com.

Fishing

You can angle for yellowtail snapper, grouper, marlin, tuna, and wahoo on deep-sea excursions. Costs range from $150 per person for a half day to $250 and up for a full day. Prices usually include bait and tackle, instruction for novices, and refreshments. Ask about licensing and insurance. Most boats give you some fillets but otherwise keep the fish, so if you want to keep yours, arrange it in advance.

Rudy's Deep Sea Fishing

FISHING | One of the more experienced sport-angling outfits runs private charter trips. Half-day excursions for up to four people start at $625. Rudy is reasonable; you can have the fillets you need and he keeps the rest. ■ TIP→ Check the website for great tips on fishing around St. Maarten. ⊠ 14 Airport Rd., Simpson Bay ☎ 721/522–7120, 721/545–2177 ⊕ www.rudysdeepseafishing.com.

Golf

Mullet Bay Golf Course

GOLF | St. Maarten is not a golf destination. Nevertheless, this golf course is 18 holes (and the island's only choice), and offers tremendous views, though it's hardly a must-play. Good clubs are available for rent, and you can wear sneakers if you don't have golf shoes with you. If you're looking for real golf, consider Anguilla, a quick 25-minute ferry ride from Marigot (passport and port fees required). There's also a nine-hole course completing development at Loterie Farm if a good, new course and incredible scenery are appealing lures. Loterie Farm offers excellent natural food as well. Caution: wild vervet monkeys will occasionally saunter across the Loterie Farm course. ⊠ Airport Rd., north of airport, Mullet Bay ☎ 721/545–2850 ⊠ $40 ⚐ 18 holes, 6200 yards, par 70.

Horseback Riding

Seaside Nature Park
HORSEBACK RIDING | FAMILY | This nature park by the sea offers hour-long horseback rides. For a romantic treat, book a sunset ride with Champagne and a bonfire (complete with marshmallows) for about $125 per person. All experience levels are welcome, as the horses only walk, but advanced riders can book private rides if they want to trot and canter. There is a discovery farm that the whole family can enjoy, a summer camp for kids, and a small restaurant on property where you can get a cold beer to drink seaside. ⊠ *64 Cay Bay Rd., Cay Bay* ☎ *721/544–5255* ⊕ *www. seasidenaturepark.com.*

Kayaking

Kayaking continues to be very popular and is frequently offered at the many water-sports operations on both the Dutch and the French sides. Rental starts at roughly $15–$20 per hour for a single and up to about $25 for a double.

★ TriSports
KAYAKING | FAMILY | This company has a full slate of reasonably priced kayaking activities, but they also offer bike tours. TriSports organizes leisurely 2½-hour combination kayaking and snorkeling excursions in addition to its biking and hiking tours. Prices vary but a fee of roughly $49 includes all equipment. ⊠ *Airport Rd., 14B, Simpson Bay* ☎ *721/545–4384* ⊕ *www.trisportsxm.com.*

Sea Excursions

★ Aqua Mania Adventures
BOATING | FAMILY | You can take day cruises to Prickly Pear Cay, off Anguilla, aboard the *Lambada,* or sunset and dinner cruises on the 65-foot sail catamaran *Tango. The Edge* goes to Saba and St. Barth. There are tours on inflatable boats, scuba and snorkel trips, and motor cruises around the island. ⊠ *Simpson Bay Beach Resort and Marina, Pelican Key* ☎ *721/544–2640, 721/544–2631* ⊕ *www.stmaarten-activities.com.*

Sail Arawak
BOATING | FAMILY | The 52-foot, competition-savvy sailing catamaran accommodates a maximum of just 12 people, enabling an intimate, enjoyable sailing experience. Arawak provides regular

full- and half-day trips in St. Maarten/St. Martin, and day trips to neighboring Anguilla. Swimming, snorkeling, and a leisurely sail are just some of what you can expect on any of the sail tours. No specific sailing experience is required since a captain and crew are onboard, but passengers can assist them and experience racing in a safe and secure way. An open bar, lunch, and snacks are offered onboard. *Arawak* is built for speed! Private charters are also available. ⊠ *Billy Folly Rd. 10, Pelican Key* ☎ *721/554-1973* ⊕ *www. sailarawaksxm.com.*

★ Celine Charters

BOATING | FAMILY | Perhaps SXM's most well-known, well-respected, and experienced captain is Neil Roebert, whose new sailing catamaran *Enigma* is docked behind Nowhere Special in Simpson Bay. Neil has a number of scheduled trips in addition to the boat's availability for charter. Whether you choose a private charter, a Fun in the Sun tour of SXM's beaches, or the Anguilla fantasy trip, you'll return relaxed and filled with great memories and quite possibly several new friends. Although Celine Charters is the name of the business (named for Neil's daughter), his current boat is named *Enigma*. Especially fun are full-day sails aboard *Enigma* which feature snorkel equipment, lunch, and top shelf drinks, all included. ⊠ *Boat is moored behind Nowhere Special in Simpson Bay, Wellfare Rd., Simpson Bay* ☎ *721/526–1170 Neil's cell phone is usually answered quickly.* ⊕ *www.sailstmaarten.com.*

Golden Eagle III

BOATING | FAMILY | Three sleek catamarans, *Golden Eagle I, II* and *III*, take day-sailors on ecofriendly excursions to outlying islets and reefs for snorkeling and partying. They can pick you up from your hotel or condo. The same company offers other boat and land tours, including the double-deck *Explorer* for cruises in Simpson Bay Lagoon. ⊠ *Bobby's Marina, Jurancho Yrausquin Bd., Philipsburg* ☎ *721/543–0068* ⊕ *www.toursxm.com.*

Snorkeling

Some of the best snorkeling on the Dutch side can be found around the rocks below Fort Amsterdam off Little Bay Beach; in the southern end of Maho Bay, near Beacon Hill; off Pelican Key; and around the reefs off the northern end of Dawn Beach, near Oyster Bay Beach Resort. On the French side, the area around Baie Orientale—including Caye Verte (Green Key) and Tintamarre—is especially beautiful and is officially classified and protected as a regional underwater nature reserve. Sea creatures also congregate around Creole Rock at the point of Baie de Grand Case, though the shallows in that area are said to offer superior snorkeling activity. The average cost of an afternoon snorkeling trip is $55–$75 per person.

Blue Bubbles

SNORKELING | FAMILY | This company offers both boat and shore snorkel excursions, ATV and Jeep tours, as well as Jet Skiing, and SNUBA for beginner divers. Snorkel excursions are $55 for two hours and $75 for four hours. ⊠ *153 Front St., Philipsburg* ☎ *721/556–8484* ⊕ *www.bluebubblessxm.com.*

Spas

Spas have added a pampering dimension to some properties on both the French and Dutch sides of the island. Be sure to book in advance, however, as walk-ins are hardly ever accommodated. There are massage cabanas on some beaches, more on the French side than the Dutch, and some of the beach clubs on Baie Orientale have a blackboard where you can sign up. Hotels that don't have spas can usually arrange in-room treatments.

★ La Samanna Spa

SPAS | You don't have to be a guest at the hotel to enjoy a treatment or a day package at this heavenly retreat, easily one of the top spas on the island. In a lovely tropical garden setting, immaculate treatment rooms feature walled gardens with private outdoor showers. There are dozens of therapies for body, face, hair, and spirit on the spa menu; any can be customized to your desires or sensitivities. ⊠ *Belmond La Samanna, Baie Longue* ☎ *0590/87–65–69* ⊕ *www.belmond.com/lasamanna* ⊗ *Closed Sun.*

ST. BARTHÉLEMY

Updated by
Sheryl Nance-Nash

● Sights	⑪ Restaurants	🛏 Hotels	● Shopping	🍸 Nightlife
★★★★☆	★★★★★	★★★★★	★★★★★	★★★★★

WELCOME TO ST. BARTHÉLEMY

TOP REASONS TO GO

★ **The Scene:** The island is active, hedonistic, and hip, and the party is always on by the sparkling-blue sea.

★ **Super Style:** Growing ever more chic, St. Barth combines French style with Caribbean flair.

★ **Great Dining:** New restaurants tempt gourmets and gourmands.

★ **Shopping Galore:** If you're a shopper, you'll find bliss stalking the latest in French clothes and accessories with prices up to 30% less than in the States.

★ **Getting Out on the Water:** Windsurfing, kitesurfing, and other water sports make going to the beach more than just a lounging experience.

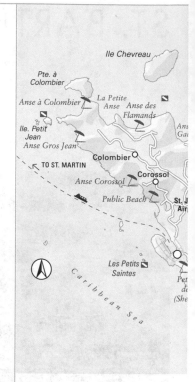

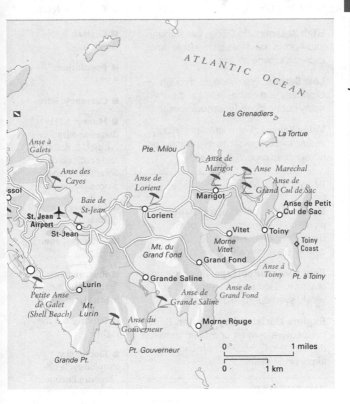

ATLANTIC OCEAN

Les Grenadiers

La Tortue

Anse à Galets

Pte. Milou

Anse de Marigot

Anse Maréchal

Anse des Cayes

Anse de Lorient

Anse de Grand Cul de Sac

ssol

Baie de St-Jean

Marigot

Anse de Petit Cul de Sac

St. Jean Airport

Lorient

St-Jean

Vitet

Toiny

Morne Vitet

Toiny Coast

Mt. du Grand Fond

Grand Fond

Lurin

Grande Saline

Anse à Toiny

Pt. à Toiny

Petite Anse de Galet (Shell Beach)

Mt. Lurin

Anse de Grande Saline

Anse de Grand Fond

Anse du Gouverneur

Morne Rouge

Pt. Gouverneur

Grande Pt.

0   1 miles

0   1 km

ISLAND SNAPSHOT

WHEN TO GO

High Season: Mid-December through mid-April is the most fashionable (and expensive) time to visit.

Low Season: From August through October the weather is hot and humid; many hotels close for renovations.

Value Season: From late April to July and again November to mid-December, hotel prices drop 20% to 30%.

WAYS TO SAVE

Picnic. Get supplies at a market and picnic on the beach to save on St. Barth's pricy restaurants. St. Barth's beaches are free and open to the public.

Rent a villa or cottage. There are some reasonable lodgings for rent by the week, even during high season.

Explore the island by scooter. Rent an inexpensive scooter or moped from rue de France in Gustavia or around the airport in St-Jean.

BIG EVENTS

January: The St. Barth Music Festival showcases music and dance. ⊕ *www. stbartsmusicfestival.org*

March: St. Barth Bucket Regatta is a three-day international regatta featuring some of the world's most incredible yachts. ⊕ *www.bucketregatta.com*

November: The St. Barth Gourmet Festival is an international gourmet food festival that brings renowned chefs to the island. ⊕ *saintbarthgourmetfestival.com*

AT A GLANCE

- **Capital:** Gustavia
- **Population:** 9,939
- **Currency:** Euro
- **Money:** ATMs dispense only euros; U.S. dollars and credit cards accepted in most places.
- **Language:** French
- **Country Code:** 590
- **Emergencies:** 18 for fire; 17 for medical and police
- **Driving:** On the right
- **Electricity:** 230v/60 cycles; plugs are European standard with two round prongs
- **Time:** Same as New York during daylight saving time; one hour ahead otherwise
- **Documents:** Up to 90 days with valid passport

St. Barthélemy blends the respective essences of the Caribbean, France, and *Architectural Digest* in perfect proportions. A sophisticated but unstudied approach to relaxation and respite prevails: you can spend the day on a beach, try on the latest French fashions, catch a gallery exhibition, and watch the sunset while nibbling tapas over Gustavia Harbor, then choose from 80 excellent restaurants for an elegant or easy evening meal. You can putter around the island, scuba dive, windsurf on a quiet cove, or just admire the lovely views.

A mere 8 square miles (21 square km), St. Barth is a hilly island, with many sheltered inlets and picturesque, quiet beaches. The town of Gustavia wraps itself around a modern harbor lined with everything from size-matters megayachts to rustic fishing boats to sailboats of all descriptions. Red-roof villas dot the hillsides, and glass-front shops line the streets. Beach surf runs the gamut from kiddie-pool calm to serious-surfer dangerous, beaches from deserted to packed. The cuisine is tops in the Caribbean, and almost everything is tidy, stylish, and up-to-date. French *savoir vivre* prevails.

Christopher Columbus came to the island—called "Ouanalao" by its native Caribs—in 1493; he named it for his brother Bartolomé. The first French colonists arrived in 1648, drawn by its location on the West Indian Trade Route, but they were wiped out by the Caribs, who dominated the area. Another small group from Normandy and Brittany arrived in 1694. This time the settlers prospered—with the help of French buccaneers, who took advantage of the island's strategic location and protected harbor. In 1784 the French traded the island to King Gustav III of Sweden in exchange for port rights in Göteborg. The king dubbed the capital Gustavia, laid out and paved streets, built three forts, and turned the community into a prosperous free port. The island thrived as a shipping and commercial center until the 19th century, when earthquakes, fires, and hurricanes brought financial ruin. Many residents fled to newer lands of opportunity, and Oscar II of Sweden returned the island to France. After briefly considering selling it to America, the French took possession of St. Barthélemy again on August 10, 1877.

Today the island is a free port, and in 2007 it became a Collectivité, a French-administered overseas territory. Arid, hilly, and rocky, St. Barth was unsuited to sugar production and thus never developed an extensive slave base. Some of the residents are descendants of the tough Norman and Breton settlers of three centuries ago, but you are more likely to encounter attractive French twenty- and thirtysomethings from Normandy and Provence, who are friendly, English-speaking, and here for the sunny lifestyle.

Planning

Getting Here and Around

AIR

Because of its tiny, hillside runway, there are no direct major-airline flights to St. Barth. Most North Americans fly first into St. Maarten's Princess Juliana International SXM Airport, from which the island is a quick 15 minutes by air. Winair has frequent flights from St. Maarten every day. Through Winair's affiliation with major airlines, you can check your luggage from your home airport through to St. Barth under certain circumstances. Tradewind Aviation has regularly scheduled service from San Juan and also does VIP charters. Anguilla Air Services and St. Barth Commuter have scheduled flights and also do charters. ■TIP➜ **Leave ample time between your scheduled flight and your connection in St. Maarten: 90 minutes is the minimum recommended** (and be aware that luggage frequently doesn't make the trip; your hotel or villa-rental company may be able to send someone to retrieve it). It's a good idea to pack a change of clothes, required medicines, and a bathing suit in your carry-on—or better yet, pack very light and don't check baggage at all.

AIRPORTS Jean Remi de Haenen (SBH). ⊠ *St. Jean Rd., St-Jean* ☎ *0590/27–75–81.*

Did You Know?

The largest hotel on St. Barth has only about 70 rooms, which means you get a great deal of personal service and attention wherever you stay.

AIRLINES St. Barth Commuter. ☎ *0590/27–54–54* ⊕ *www.stbarth-commuter.com.* **Tradewind Aviation.** ☎ *203/267–3305* ⊕ *www.fly-tradewind.com.* **Trans Anguilla Airways.** ☎ *264/498–5922* ⊕ *www.transanguilla.com.* **Winair.** ☎ *0590/27–61–01, 866/545-4237* ⊕ *www.fly-winair.com.*

BOAT AND FERRY

St. Barth can be reached via ferry service from St. Maarten/St. Martin to Quai de la République in Gustavia. Voyager offers at least twice daily round-trips for about $100, economy class per person from Marigot. Great Bay Express has multiple round-trips daily from the Dutch side of Sint Maarten for roughly €110 if reserved in advance, €115 for same-day tickets, and €70 each way for a same-day round-trip. Private boat charters are also available, but they are very expensive; MasterSki Pilou offers transfers from St. Maarten.

CONTACTS Great Bay Express. ✉ *Quai Gustavia, Gustavia* ☎ *721/520–5015* ⊕ *www.greatbayexpress.com.* **Master Ski Pilou.** ☎ *0590/27–91–79* ⊕ *www.masterski-pilou.com.* **Voyager.** ☎ *0590/87–10–68* ⊕ *www.voy12.com.*

CAR

Roads are sometimes unmarked, so get a map and look for signs, nailed to posts at all crossroads, pointing to a destination. Roads are narrow and sometimes very steep, but have been improved; even so, check the brakes and low gears before driving away from the rental office. Maximum speed is 30 mph (50 kph). Driving is on the right, as in the United States and Europe. Parking is an additional challenge. There are two gas stations on the island, one near the airport and one in Lorient. They aren't open after 5 pm or on Sunday, and pumps at the station near the airport now accept chip-and-pin credit cards. Considering the short distances, a full tank should last most of a week.

■**TIP**→ **Ask your car rental company about Blue Parking Tags, which give you 1½ hours of parking for free.**

Car Rentals: You must have a valid driver's license and be 25 or older to rent, and in high season there may be a three-day minimum. During peak periods, such as Christmas week and February, arrange for your car rental ahead of time. Rental agencies operate out of Jean Remi de Haenen airport; some will bring your car to your hotel. Alternately, when you make your hotel reservation, ask if the hotel has its own cars available to rent; some hotels provide 24-hour emergency road service—something most rental companies don't. Expect to pay at least $55 per day, and note the company will usually hold about $500 until the car is returned.

■ TIP→ For a green alternative, consider renting an electric car. They're available for about $85 per day.

MOPED, SCOOTER, AND BIKE

Several companies rent motorbikes, scooters, mopeds, ATVs, and mountain bikes. Motorbikes go for about $30 per day and require a $100 deposit. ATV rental starts at $40 per day. Helmets are required. Scooter and motorbike rental places are mostly along rue de France in Gustavia and around the airport in St-Jean. If you have not driven an ATV or "quad" before, St. Barth may not be the best place to try it out. The roads, though not jammed with traffic, are quite narrow, and navigating the hilly terrain can be quite a challenge.

CONTACTS Barthloc Rental. ⊠ *Rue de France, Gustavia* ☎ *0590/27–52–81* ⊕ *www.barthloc.com*. **Chez Béranger.** ⊠ *21 rue du général de Gaulle, Gustavia* ☎ *0590/27–89–00* ⊕ *www.beranger-rental. com.*

TAXI

Taxis are expensive and not particularly easy to arrange, especially in the evening. There's a taxi station at the airport and another at the ferry dock in Gustavia; from elsewhere you must contact a dispatcher in Gustavia or St-Jean. Fares are regulated by the Collectivity, and drivers accept both dollars and euros. If you go out to dinner by taxi, let the restaurant know if you will need a taxi at the end of the meal, and they will call one for you.

CONTACTS Taxi Prestige. ☎ *0590/27–70–57.*

Beaches

There is a beach in St. Barth to suit every taste. Wild surf, complete privacy in nature, a dreamy white-sand strand, and a spot at a chic beach club close to shopping and restaurants—they're all within a 20-minute drive.

There are many *anses* (coves) and nearly 20 *plages* (beaches) scattered around the island, each with a distinct personality; all are open to the public, even if they front a tony resort. Because of the number of beaches, even in high season you can find a nearly empty one, despite St. Barth's tiny size. That's not to say that all beaches are equally good or even equally suitable for swimming, but each has something to offer. Unless you are having lunch at a beachfront restaurant with lounging areas set aside for patrons, you should bring an umbrella, beach mat, and drinking water (all of which are easily obtainable all over the island). Topless sunbathing is common, but nudism is *supposedly* forbidden—although both Grande Saline and Gouverneur are de facto nude beaches, albeit less than in the past. Shade is scarce.

Restaurants

Dining on St. Barth compares favorably to almost anywhere in the world. Varied and exquisite cuisine, a French flair in the decor, sensational wine, and attentive service make for a wonderful epicurean experience. On most menus, freshly caught local seafood mingles on the plate with top-quality provisions that arrive regularly from Paris. Interesting selections on the Cartes de Vins are no surprise, but don't miss the sophisticated cocktails whipped up by island bartenders. The signature drink of St. Barth is called "'ti punch," a rum concoction similar to a Brazilian caipirinha. *Ti creux* means "snack" or "small bite."

Reservations are strongly recommended and, in high season, essential. At the end of the meal, as in France, you must request the bill. Until you do, you can feel free to linger at the table.

Check restaurant bills carefully. A *service compris* (service charge) is always added by law, but you should leave the server 5% to 10% extra in cash. You'll usually come out ahead if you charge restaurant meals on a credit card in euros instead of paying with American currency, as your credit card might offer a better exchange rate than the restaurant (unless your credit card adds a conversion surcharge).

In menu prices below, lobster has been left out of the range.

What to Wear: A bathing suit and gauzy top or shift is acceptable at beachside lunch spots, but not really in Gustavia. St. Barth is for fashionistas. You can't go wrong in a tank dress or a nice top with white jeans, high sandals, and flashy accessories. The sky is the limit for high fashion at nightclubs and lounges in high season, when you might (correctly) think everyone in sight is a model. Jackets are never required and are rarely worn, but most people do dress fashionably for dinner. Leave some space in your suitcase; you can buy the perfect outfit here on the island. Pack a light sweater or shawl for the occasional breezy night.

Restaurant prices are the average cost of a main course at dinner or, if dinner is not served, at lunch. Restaurant reviews have been shortened. For full information, visit Fodors.com.

Hotels and Resorts

There's no denying that hotel rooms and villas on St. Barth carry high prices. You're paying primarily for the privilege of staying on the island, and even at $1,000 a night the bedrooms tend to be small. Still, if you're flexible—in terms of timing and in your choice of lodgings—you can enjoy a holiday in St. Barth and still afford to send the kids to college.

The most expensive season falls during the holidays (December 26 to January 2), when hotels are booked far in advance, may require a 10- or 14-day stay, and can be double the high-season rates. A 5% government tourism tax on room prices (excluding breakfast) is in effect; be sure to ask if it is included in your room rate or added on.

Small luxury hotels: The largest hotel on the island has 66 rooms, but the majority are stratospherically expensive.

Villas: Private villas provide 2,500 rooms and hotels 500 rooms.

Hotel prices are the lowest cost of a standard double room in high season. Hotel reviews have been shortened. For full information, visit Fodors.com.

What It Costs in Euros

	$	$$	$$$	$$$$
RESTAURANTS				
	under €12	€12–€20	€21–€30	over €30
HOTELS				
	under €275	€275–€375	€376–€475	over €475

PRIVATE VILLAS AND CONDOS

On St. Barth the term *villa* describes anything from a small cottage to a luxurious, modern estate. Today more than half of St. Barth's accommodations are in villas, a great option, especially if traveling with friends or family. Even more advantageous to Americans, villa rates are usually quoted in dollars, thus bypassing unfavorable euro fluctuations. Most villas have a small private swimming pool and maid service daily except Sunday. They are well furnished with linens, kitchen utensils, and such electronic necessities as smart-phone docks, TV, and Internet. Weekly low-season rates range from $3,000 + to "oh-my-gosh." Some villa-rental companies also have offices in the United States and have extensive websites that enable you to see pictures or panoramic videos of the place you're considering; their local offices oversee maintenance and housekeeping and provide concierge services. Just be aware that there are few beachfront villas, so if you have your heart set on "toes in the sand" and a cute waiter delivering your Kir Royale, stick with the hotels or villas operated by hotel properties.

Nightlife

Most of the nightlife in St. Barth is centered in Gustavia, though there are a few places to go outside of town. "In" clubs change from season to season, so you might ask around for the hot spot of the moment, but none really get going until about midnight. Theme parties are the current trend. Check the daily *St. Barth News* or *Le Journal de Saint-Barth* for details. A late (10 pm or later) reservation at one of the club–restaurants will eventually become a front-row seat at a party.

Shopping

St. Barth is a duty-free port, and its sophisticated visitors find shopping in its 200-plus boutiques a delight, especially for beachwear, accessories, jewelry, and casual wear. It's no overstatement to say that shopping for fashionable clothing, jewels, and designer accessories is better in St. Barth than anywhere else in the Caribbean. New shops open all the time, so there's always something to discover. Some stores close from noon to 3, but they are open until 8 pm. Many are closed on Sunday. A popular afternoon pastime is strolling the two major shopping areas in Gustavia and St-Jean. While high fashion is as pricey here as everywhere, French brands sell for up to 30% less than in the U.S.

Health and Safety

There's relatively little crime on St. Barth. Visitors can travel anywhere on the island with confidence. Most hotel rooms have safes for your valuables. As anywhere, don't tempt loss by leaving cameras, laptops, or jewelry out in plain sight in your hotel room or villa or in your car or car trunk. Also, don't walk barefoot at night: there are venomous centipedes that can inflict a remarkably painful sting. If you ask residents, they will tell you that they drink only bottled water, although most cook or make coffee with tap water.

Dengue, chikungunya, and Zika have all been reported throughout the Caribbean. We recommend that you protect yourself from these mosquito-borne illnesses by keeping your skin covered and/or wearing mosquito repellent. The mosquitoes that transmit these viruses are as active by day as they are by night. Small hand-held mosquito zappers are available in some supermarkets.

Backup Ferry

Even if you are flying to St. Barth, it's a good idea to keep the numbers and schedules for the ferry companies handy, in case your flight is delayed. If you are planning to spend time in St. Maarten before traveling on to St. Barth, the ferry may be lower in cost, and you can leave from Marigot or Philipsburg.

Visitor Information

CONTACT St Barts Office du Tourisme. ⊠ *10 rue de France, Gustavia* ☎ *0590/27–87–27* ⊕ *www. saintbarth-tourisme.com.*

Gustavia

You can easily explore all of Gustavia during a two-hour stroll. Some shops close from noon to 3 or 4, so plan lunch accordingly, but stores stay open past 7 in the evening. Parking in Gustavia is a challenge, especially during vacation times. A good spot to park is rue de la République, alongside the catamarans, yachts, and sailboats.

◉ Sights

★ Le Musée Territorial, Wall House

HISTORY MUSEUM | FAMILY | On the far side of the harbor known as La Pointe, the charming Municipal Museum on the first floor of the restored Wall House has watercolors, portraits, photographs, traditional costumes, and historic documents detailing the island's history over many hundreds of years, as well as displays of the island's flowers, plants, and marine life. There are also changing contemporary art exhibitions. It's a must-stop on your St. Barth visit, and it's free. ⊠ *La Pointe, Gustavia* ☎ *0590/29–71–55* ⊕ *visit-ersaintbarthelemy.com/musee-territorial-de-gustavia* ⊠ *Free.*

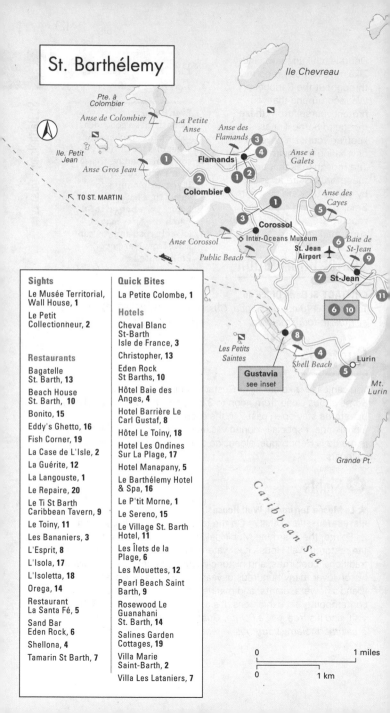

St. Barthélemy

Ile Chevreau

Pte. à Colombier

Anse de Colombier

La Petite Anse

Anse des Flamands

Flamands

Anse à Galets

Ile Petit Jean

Anse Gros Jean

← TO ST. MARTIN

Colombier

Anse des Cayes

Corossol

◇ Inter-Oceans Museum

Anse Corossol

Public Beach

St. Jean Airport

Baie de St-Jean

St-Jean

Les Petits Saintes

Gustavia see inset

Shell Beach

Lurin

Mt. Lurin

Grande Pt.

Caribbean Sea

Sights

Le Musée Territorial, Wall House, **1**

Le Petit Collectionneur, **2**

Restaurants

Bagatelle St. Barth, **13**

Beach House St. Barth, **10**

Bonito, **15**

Eddy's Ghetto, **16**

Fish Corner, **19**

La Case de L'Isle, **2**

La Guérite, **12**

La Langouste, **1**

Le Repaire, **20**

Le Ti St Barth Caribbean Tavern, **9**

Le Toiny, **11**

Les Bananiers, **3**

L'Esprit, **8**

L'Isola, **17**

L'Isoletta, **18**

Orega, **14**

Restaurant La Santa Fé, **5**

Sand Bar Eden Rock, **6**

Shellona, **4**

Tamarin St Barth, **7**

Quick Bites

La Petite Colombe, **1**

Hotels

Cheval Blanc St-Barth Isle de France, **3**

Christopher, **13**

Eden Rock St Barths, **10**

Hôtel Baie des Anges, **4**

Hotel Barrière Le Carl Gustaf, **8**

Hôtel Le Toiny, **18**

Hotel Les Ondines Sur La Plage, **17**

Hotel Manapany, **5**

Le Barthélemy Hotel & Spa, **16**

Le P'tit Morne, **1**

Le Sereno, **15**

Le Village St. Barth Hotel, **11**

Les Îlets de la Plage, **6**

Les Mouettes, **12**

Pearl Beach Saint Barth, **9**

Rosewood Le Guanahani St. Barth, **14**

Salines Garden Cottages, **19**

Villa Marie Saint-Barth, **2**

Villa Les Lataniers, **7**

| 0 | | 1 miles |
| 0 | | 1 km |

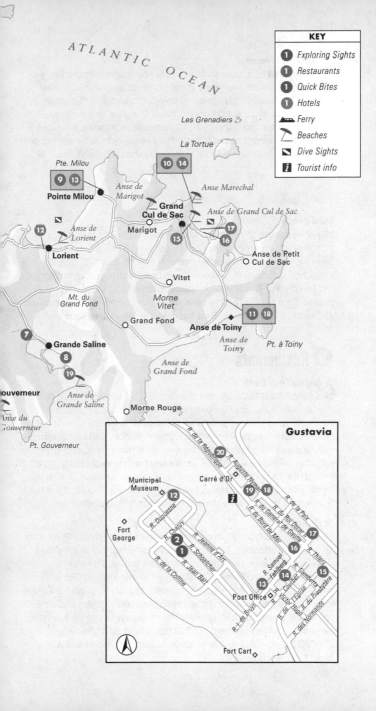

ATLANTIC OCEAN

Les Grenadiers

La Tortue

KEY

- ❶ Exploring Sights
- ❶ Restaurants
- ❶ Quick Bites
- ❶ Hotels
- Ferry
- Beaches
- Dive Sights
- 𝒊 Tourist info

Pte. Milou

❾ ❶❸
Pointe Milou

Anse de Marigot

❿ ⑭

Grand Cul de Sac

Anse Marechal

Anse de Grand Cul de Sac

⑫

Anse de Lorient

Lorient

Marigot

⑮

⑰
⑯

Anse de Petit Cul de Sac

Vitet

Mt. du Grand Fond

Morne Vitet

Grand Fond

Anse de Toiny

⑪ ⑱

Anse de Toiny

Pt. à Toiny

❼

Grande Saline

❽

⑲

Anse de Grand Fond

Gouverneur

Anse de Grande Saline

Morne Rouge

Anse du Gouverneur

Pt. Gouverneur

Gustavia

R. de la Republique

⑳ R. Auguste Nyman

Carré d'Or

Municipal Museum

R. Duquesne

⑫

R. Chanzy

❷

R. Jeanne d'Arc

❶

R. Schoelcher

Fort George

R. de la Colline

R. Jean Bart

⑲ ⑱

R. du Roi Oscar II

R. du General de Gaulle

R. du Bord de Mer

R. de la Paix

⑰

⑯

R. Thiers

R. Samuel Fahlberg

⑭

R. Gambetta

⑮

⑬

Post Office

R. Courbet

R. Victor Hugo

R. de l'Eglise

R. du Presbytère

R. des Normands

R. L. de Bruyn

Fort Cart

Le Petit Collectionneur

OTHER MUSEUM | Encouraged by family and friends, André Berry opened this private museum in his home to showcase his lifelong passion for collecting fascinating objects such as 18th-century English pipes and the first phonograph to come to the island. Today there are more than 1,000 pieces here, ranging from cannon balls to coins that are hundreds of years old. Berry will happily show you his treasures. ⊠ *La Pointe, Gustavia* ☎ *0590/27-67-77* 🎫 *€2.*

Beaches

Shell Beach

BEACH | Because of its rather sheltered southward-facing location on the coast south of downtown Gustavia, this small beach sees high numbers of shells washing ashore. Despite that, the unspoken rule here is "Take nothing but pictures, leave nothing but footprints." A taxi will be happy to take you here, but for most people it's a relatively easy walk. Have lunch at Shellona for music and relaxed island vibes. **Best for:** walking. **Amenities:** food and drink; restrooms. ⊠ *Gustavia.*

 Restaurants

★ Bagatelle St Barth

$$$$ | **MODERN FRENCH** | Watch the yachts on Gustavia harbor from the terrace of this sophisticated St-Tropez–inspired restaurant while enjoying cocktails and French and Mediterranean cuisine. Fans of sister establishments in Dubai, London, and elsewhere will recognize the friendly service, lively atmosphere, and great music provided by resident DJs. **Known for:** late-night partying; chic crowd; haute cuisine in an elegant harborside location. ⑤ *Average main: €45* ⊠ *24 Rue Samuel Fahlberg, Gustavia* ☎ *0590/27–51–51* ⊕ *www.bistrotbagatelle.com* ☾ *Closed Sun. No lunch.*

★ Bonito

$$$$ | **LATIN AMERICAN** | Combining cuisines from France, Peru, and all over the Americas, Bonito delivers a spectrum of artistically assembled flavors, textures, and aromas that you'd find challenging to locate elsewhere. Located on a hill overlooking Gustavia harbor, the restaurant indulges you with big white canvas couches for lounging, tables around the sides, an open kitchen, and three bar areas. **Known for:** caring owners; artistically presented dishes; elegance. ⑤ *Average main: €60* ⊠ *Rue Lubin Brin, Gustavia* ☎ *0590/27–96–96* ⊕ *www.ilovebonito.com* ☾ *Closed late Aug.– Nov. 1, no lunch.*

Gustavia Harbor welcomes ships to St. Barth.

Eddy's Ghetto

$$$ | FRENCH | By local standards, dinner in the pretty, open-air, tropical garden here is reasonably priced. The cooking is French and Creole, and everything is fresh and delicious. **Known for:** attentive service regardless of how busy they are; authentic French and local dishes; beautiful tropical gardens. $ *Average main: €28* ✉ *12 rue Samuel Fahlberg, Gustavia* ☎ *0590/27–54–17* ☽ *Closed Sun. and Sept. through late Oct. No lunch.*

Fish Corner

$$$$ | MEDITERRANEAN | This comfy, intimate spot, noted for its lobster tank, serves mostly local fish with Caribbean flair. You'll have a hard time deciding between the fish tacos, tuna burgers on sesame brioche bun, lobster risotto, or Chilean sea bass with white bean velouté truffle oil. **Known for:** relaxed vibe; fresh veggies; adjacent fish market. $ *Average main: €32* ✉ *41 rue de la Republic, Gustavia* ☎ *0590/51–36–33* ⊕ *www.instagram.com/ fishcornerstbarth* ☽ *Closed Sun., no dinner except Thurs.–Sat.*

La Guérite

$$$$ | MEDITERRANEAN | A sister of a well-beloved Cannes hot spot, this stylish Greek-influenced restaurant is at the far side of Gustavia Harbor. The room is beautiful, overlooking the yachts; the service helpful and friendly; and the food is fresh, tasty, healthy, and well prepared, featuring many locally caught types of seafood. **Known for:** wahoo, sea bass, mahimahi, and tuna entrées; Black

Angus rib eye; fish or veal Milanaise. $ *Average main: €45* ⊠ *La Pointe, Gustavia* ☎ *0590/27-71-83* ⊕ *www.saint-barth.restaurantlaguerite.com.*

Le Repaire

$$$ | BRASSERIE | FAMILY | Overlooking the harbor, this friendly classic French brasserie is busy from its 7 am opening to its late-night closing. The flexible hours are great if you arrive on the island midafternoon and need a substantial snack. **Known for:** reliable any time of day; well-prepared, simple food; St. Barth's only early breakfast restaurant. $ *Average main: €30* ⊠ *Rue de la République, Gustavia* ☎ *0590/27-72-48.*

★ L'Isola

$$$$ | ITALIAN | The chic sister of Santa Monica, California's Via Veneto packs in happy guests for classic Italian dishes, dozens of house-made pasta dishes, prime meats, and a huge, well-chosen wine list. Restaurateur Fabrizio Bianconi wants it to feel like a big Italian party, and with all the celebrating in this pretty and romantic room, he has certainly succeeded. **Known for:** festive atmosphere; the daily catch; house-made pasta. $ *Average main: €45* ⊠ *rue du Roi Oscar II, Gustavia* ☎ *0590/51–00–05* ⊕ *www.lisolastbarth.com* ☉ *Closed Sept. and Oct. No lunch.*

L'Isoletta

$$$$ | PIZZA | This casual Roman-style pizzeria run by the popular L'Isola restaurant is a lively, chic lounge-style gastropub serving delicious thin-crust pizzas by the slice or the meter. There are even dessert pizzas, and excellent tiramisu. **Known for:** lively atmosphere; wait times at peak hours; meter-long pizzas. $ *Average main: €38* ⊠ *Rue du Roi Oscar II, Gustavia* ☎ *0590/52–02–02* ⊕ *www.lisolettastbarth.com.*

★ Orega

$$$$ | JAPANESE FUSION | One of St. Barth's very best, this Franco-Japanese fusion restaurant draws legions of admirers for its top-notch sushi and fish, imported directly from sushi markets in

Tokyo, New York, and Paris. The pretty room in which it's served is decorated in natural woods, neutral linen, and attractive art. **Known for:** outstanding service; Franço-Japanese fusions like Pomme Shiso; extraordinary sushi and fish. ⑤ *Average main: €54* ✉ *13 rue Samuel Fahlberg, Gustavia* ☎ *0590/52–45–31* ⊕ *www. oregastbarth.com* ⊗ *Closed Sun.*

★ Shellona

$$$$ | GREEK | The sounds of Ibiza and Mykonos, in the form of live bands and DJs, fill the air at Shellona as patrons chill with a cocktail on comfortable couches and sunbeds. Lunch here is all about Greek sharing dishes with a side of Caribbean Sea views. **Known for:** music on the beach; grilled meats with herbs; cocktails. ⑤ *Average main: €47* ✉ *Shell Beach, Gustavia* ☎ *0590/29–06 66* ⊕ *shellonabeach.com* ⊗ *No dinner.*

 ## Hotels

★ Hôtel Barrière Le Carl Gustaf

$$$$ | HOTEL | The only hotel on the island with panoramic views of the port of Gustavia, this sophisticated hillside hotel is the last word in luxury and French-style charm. **Pros:** beautiful spa; close to Shell Beach, the port, shopping, and attractions; excellent restaurant. **Cons:** not budget-friendly; on a hill; not on the beach. ⑤ *Rooms from: €1100* ✉ *rue des Normands, Gustavia* ☎ *0590/29–79–00* ⊕ *www.hotelsbarriere.com* ⊗ *Closed late Aug.–late Oct.* ⤵ *21 rooms* ⑪ *Free Breakfast.*

 ## Nightlife

Bar de l'Oubli

BARS | Locals and visitors mingle over drinks at this landmark bar, which is a good breakfast option, too. The service can be slow, though, so it's best if you're not in a hurry. ✉ *3 Rue de la France, Gustavia* ☎ *0590/27–70–06* ⊕ *www.bardeloubli.com* ⌐ *No credit cards.*

Le Repaire

BARS | This restaurant lures a crowd for cocktail hour and its pool table. It's great for dinner and people-watching. ✉ *Rue de la République, Gustavia* ☎ *0590/27–72–48.*

★ Le Sélect

GATHERING PLACES | Quite possibly the inspiration for Jimmy Buffett's "Cheeseburger in Paradise," St. Barth's original hangout has been around since 1949. In the boisterous garden, the barefoot boating set gathers for a cold Carib beer at lower-than-usual prices while listening to a local band or DJ. And yes, you can grab a legendary "Cheeseburger in Paradise" here and not get indigestion when you see the surprisingly modest bill. ⊠ *Rue de la France, Gustavia* 🕾 *0590/27–86–87.*

🛍 Shopping

In Gustavia, boutiques pack the three major shopping streets. Quai de la République, which is right on the harbor, rivals New York's Madison Avenue or Paris's avenue Montaigne for high-end designer retail, including shops for **Louis Vuitton, Bulgari, Cartier, Chopard, Erès,** and **Hermès.** These shops often carry items that are not available in the United States. The elegant Carré d'Or plaza and the adjacent **Coeur Ven dôme** are great fun to explore. Shops are also clustered in **La Savane Commercial Center** (across from the airport), **La Villa Créole** (in St-Jean), and **Espace Neptune** (on the road to Lorient). It's worth working your way from one end to the other at these shopping complexes—just to see or, perhaps, be seen. Boutiques in all three areas carry the latest in French and Italian sportswear, charming children's togs, and some haute couture. Bargains may be tough to come by, but you might be able to snag that Birkin that has a long waiting list stateside, and in any case, you'll have a lot of fun hunting around.

BOOKS
Clic
BOOKS | Devoted to books on photography and monthly exhibits of fine modern photography, as well as arty things to wear, this concept gallery–bookstore is an outpost of those in SoHo (New York) and the Hamptons. It's the brainchild of Calypso founder Christiane Celle. ⊠ *Rue de la République, Gustavia* 🕾 *0590/29–70–17* ⊕ *www.clic.com* ☾ *Closed Sun.*

La Case Aux Livres
BOOKS | This full-service bookstore and newsstand has hundreds of English titles for adults and kids. Its blog lists author appearances, which may well be worth a stop if you're around. ⊠ *9 rue de la République, Gustavia* 🕾 *0590/27–15–88* ⊕ *www.lacaseauxlivres. com.*

CLOTHING
Boutique Lacoste
MIXED CLOTHING | This store has a huge selection of the once-again-chic alligator-logo wear for adults and kids. ⊠ *Rue du Bord de Mer, Gustavia* 🕾 *0590/27–66–90.*

Shoppers flock to Gustavia's Rue de France for high-end boutiques.

Hermès

MIXED CLOTHING | This independently owned franchise (closed September and October) has prices slightly below those in the States, a welcome notion among the sky-high prices here. ⊠ *Le Carré d'Or, Gustavia* ☎ *0590/27–66–15* ⊙ *Closed Sun.*

Kokon

MIXED CLOTHING | This boutique offers a nicely edited mix of designs for on-island or off from of-the-moment fashion lines, and cute shoes to go with them. ⊠ *Rue Samuel Fahlberg, Gustavia* ☎ *0590/29–74–48.*

Laurent Effel

MIXED CLOTHING | This St. Barth institution operates three attractive shops next to each other, offering comfy and colorful driving mocs for adults, well-tailored linen shirts and shorts in a rainbow of candy colors, and accessories. ⊠ *Rue du Générale de Gaulle, Gustavia* ☎ *0590/27–54–02.*

Linen

MEN'S CLOTHING | This shop offers tailored linen shirts for men in a rainbow of soft colors and soft slip-on driving mocs in classic styles. ⊠ *Rue du Générale de Gaulle, Gustavia* ☎ *0590/27–54–26* ⊕ *www.facebook.com/Linensbh.*

L.Joy Boutique

MIXED CLOTHING | Look for lovely high-end silk tunics, evening wear, and elegant accessories. Brides-to-be and the glitter/

sparkle-obsessed should not miss the collection of beaded and rhinestone-set headbands and sparkly sandals. ⊠ *Rue du Bord de Mer* ☎ *0590/27–14–89* ⊕ *www.facebook.com/ljoyboutique.*

Lolita Jaca

MIXED CLOTHING | This store has trendy, tailored sportswear and floaty silk charmeuse and cotton gauze tunics perfect for the beach. ⊠ *Le Carré d'Or, Gustavia* ☎ *0590/27–59–98* ⊕ *www. lolitajaca.com.*

Mademoiselle Hortense

MIXED CLOTHING | Charming tops and dresses in pretty prints are made on the island. Great crafty bracelets and necklaces to accent your new styles are also here. ⊠ *Rue de la République, Gustavia* ☎ *0590/27–13–29.*

PaSha St Barth

MIXED CLOTHING | PaSha St. Barth's concept store stocks cheeky slogan T-shirts, swimsuits, edgy hats, gifts, and accessories for adults. ⊠ *14 Rue Oscar II, Gustavia* ☎ *0590/39–01–99.*

Pati de St Barth

MIXED CLOTHING | This is the largest of the three shops that stock the chic, locally made T-shirts, totes, and beach wraps that have become the de facto logo of St. Barth. The newest styles have hand-done graffiti-style lettering. The shop also has some handicrafts and other giftable items. ⊠ *Rue du Bord de Mer, Gustavia* ☎ *0590/27–78–04* ⊕ *www.patidestbarth.com.*

Poupette St. Barth

MIXED CLOTHING | All the brilliant color-crinkle silk, chiffon batik, and embroidered peasant skirts and tops are designed by the owner. There also are great belts and beaded bracelets. ⊠ *Rue de la République, Gustavia* ☎ *0590/27–94-49* ⊕ *www.poupettestbarth. com.*

Saint-Barth Stock Exchange

MIXED CLOTHING | On the far side of Gustavia Harbor, the island's consignment and discount shop is a blast to explore. ⊠ *Rue Schoelcher, La Pointe, Gustavia* ☎ *0590/27–68–12.*

Vanita Rosa

MIXED CLOTHING | This store showcases beautiful lace and linen sundresses and peasant tops, plus poncho/kaftans, accessories galore, and very cool designer vintage. ⊠ *Rue Oscar II, Gustavia* ☎ *0590/87-46-91* ⊕ *www.vanitarosa.com* ⊙ *Closed Sun.*

Voila St Barth

MIXED CLOTHING | Find beautifully made linen and cotton resort sportswear mostly in a classic blue-and-white palette at this polished shop. The classic styles are wearable by all ages. There is a sister shop in St-Jean. ⊠ *4 rue de la Suède, Gustavia* ☎ *0590/27–99–53* ⊕ *www.voilastbarth-shop.com/en/.*

Volver St Barth

MIXED CLOTHING | The attractive shop stocks a fashion-forward selection by SeeByChloé, Alexander Wang, ba&sh, forte_forte, Lisa Marie Fernandez, Thurley, and remarkable folkloric, one-of-a-kind garments. ⊠ *Rue de France, Gustavia* ☎ *0590/27–55–90* ⊕ *www.volverstbarth.com.*

FOODSTUFFS

AMC

FOOD | This supermarket is a bit older than Marché U in St-Jean but can supply nearly anything you might need. ⊠ *Quai de la République, Gustavia* ☎ *0590/27–52–00* ⊗ *Closed Sun.* ⌦ *Additional locations in Lorient and St.-Jean.*

JEWELRY

Cartier

JEWELRY & WATCHES | For fine jewelry, visit this branch of the famous jeweler. ⊠ *Quai de la République, Gustavia* ☎ *0590/27–66–69* ⊕ *stores.cartier.com/france/st-barthelemy/quai-de-la-republique-gustavia* ⊗ *Closed Sun.*

Diamond Genesis

JEWELRY & WATCHES | A good selection of watches, including Patek Philippe and Chanel, can be found at this store. Pendants and charms in the shape of the island, available in gold, are popular purchases, as are high-end jewels by Graff and Pomellato. ⊠ *Rue de la République, Gustavia* ☎ *0590/27–66–94* ⊕ *www.diamondgenesis.com.*

Fabienne Miot

JEWELRY & WATCHES | Unusual and artistic jewelry features rare stones and cultured pearls, watches, and jewelry. ⊠ *Rue de la République, Gustavia* ☎ *0590/27–73–13* ⊕ *www.fabiennemiot.com.*

Kalinas Perles

JEWELRY & WATCHES | Beautiful freshwater pearls are knotted onto the classic St. Barth–style leather thongs by artist Jérémy Albaledejo, who also showcases other artisans' works. Tahitian black pearls are featured. ⊠ *23 rue du Général de Gaulle, Gustavia* ☎ *0690/65–93–00* ⊕ *www.kalinasperles.com.*

Time

JEWELRY & WATCHES | This store specializes in exclusive watches by Breitling, Bell and Ross, Giuliano Mazzuoli, BRM, Boucheron, and more. ⊠ *Rue de la République, Gustavia* ☏ *0590/27–99–10* ⊕ *www.access.sb/en/st-barts/shopping/watchmakers/time.*

LEATHER GOODS AND ACCESSORIES
Human Steps

SHOES | This popular boutique stocks a well-edited selection of chic shoes and leather accessories from names like YSL, Givenchy, Balenciaga, Miu Miu, and Jimmy Choo. ⊠ *39 rue de la République, Gustavia* ☏ *0590/27–93–79* ⊕ *www.human-steps.fr.*

LIQUOR AND TOBACCO
Couleurs des Iles 120% Lino

TOBACCO | This shop has many rare varieties of smokables, including Cuban cigars, plus the original Panama hats, and good souvenir T-shirts, too. Head to the back for the stash of rare Puro Vintage. ⊠ *Rue du Général de Gaulle, Gustavia* ☏ *0590/27–79–20.*

La Cave du Port Franc

WINE/SPIRITS | This store has a huge selection of wine, especially from France. ⊠ *Rue de la République, Gustavia* ☏ *0590/27–65–27* ⊕ *www.lacaveduportfranc.com.*

M'Bolo

WINE/SPIRITS | Sample infused rums, including lemongrass, ginger, and the island favorite, vanilla, and bring some home in beautiful handblown bottles. Laguiole knives and local spices are sold, too, plus artisan products like homemade jam. ⊠ *Rue du Général de Gaulle, Gustavia* ☏ *0590/27–90–54* ⊕ *mbolo-rum.com/en.*

Anse de Toiny

Over the hills beyond Grand Cul de Sac is this much-photographed coastline. Stone fences crisscross the steep slopes of Morne du Vitet, one of many small mountains on St. Barth, along a rocky shore that resembles the rugged coast of Normandy. Nicknamed the "washing machine" because of its turbulent surf, it is not recommended even to expert swimmers because of the strong undertow.

■ **TIP→ There is a tough but scenic hike around the point. Take the road past Le Toiny hotel to the top to the start of the trail.**

Restaurants

Le Toiny

$$$$ | MODERN FRENCH | Hôtel Le Toiny's dramatic cliffside dining porch showcases nature and gastronomy in equal parts. The food is notable for its innovation and extraordinary presentation, and the warm but consummately professional service sets a high standard. **Known for:** attention to detail; relaxing setting; exquisite views. $ *Average main: €50* ⊠ *Hôtel Le Toiny, Anse de Toiny* 🕿 *0590/27–88–88* ⊕ *www.letoiny.com* ⊗ *Closed Sept.–mid-Oct.*

🛏 Hotels

★ Hôtel Le Toiny

$$$$ | HOTEL | The privacy, serenity, and personalized service at this remote, beachy chic hotel will make you never want to leave. **Pros:** suites have private pool and outdoor shower; lovely alfresco restaurant; environmental awareness. **Cons:** pricey, as are most St. Barth properties; must take a hotel shuttle to reach the beach (though they're readily available); isolated (at least half an hour's drive from town). $ *Rooms from: €1980* ⊠ *Anse de Toiny* 🕿 *0590/27–88–88* ⊕ *www.letoiny.com* ⊗ *Closed Sept.–late Oct.* 🛌 *22 suites* ⦿ *Free Breakfast.*

Colombier

Beaches

Anse de Colombier

BEACH | The beach here is the island's least accessible, thus the most private; to reach it you must take either a rocky footpath from Petite Anse or brave the 30-minute climb down (and back up) a steep, cactus-bordered trail from the top of the mountain behind the beach. Appropriate footgear is a must, and on the beach, the only shade is a rock cave. But this is a good place to snorkel. Boaters favor this cove for its calm anchorage. **Amenities:** none. **Best for:** snorkeling; swimming. ⊠ *Colombier.*

🍴 Restaurants

Les Bananiers

$$$ | FRENCH | FAMILY | Ask the locals where to eat, and they will surely recommend this casual spot in Colombier, adjacent to a wonderful bakery. The food is classic French (though they're also

Dinner at Le Toiny is private and romantic.

well-known for pizza), the service is warm, the prices are gentle (a rarity here), and you can eat in or take out. **Known for:** reasonable prices; a can't-miss bakery next door; thin-crust pizza. ⑤ *Average main: €26* ⊠ *Rte. de Colombier, Colombier* ☎ *0590/27–93–48.*

Coffee and Quick Bites

La Petite Colombe

$ | **BAKERY** | If you're in Colombier (or Lorient, where there's a second location) pop into La Petite for pastries, bread, and baguettes that are the stuff of dreams. You can grab and go or sit for a spell here. **Known for:** sandwiches and salads; picnic fixings; coffee and baked goodies. ⑤ *Average main: €10* ⊠ *D209, Colombier* ☎ *0590/29–74–30 Lorient, 0590/27–95–27 Colombier* ⊕ *www. facebook.com/petitecolombestbarth* ☉ *No dinner.*

🛏 Hotels

Le P'tit Morne

$ | **B&B/INN** | Each of the modestly furnished but clean and freshly decorated, painted mountainside studios has a private balcony with panoramic views of the coastline. **Pros:** reasonable rates; great area for hiking; helpful management. **Cons:** remote location; not on the beach; rooms are basic. ⑤ *Rooms from: €231* ⊠ *Colombier* ☎ *0590/52–95–50* ⊕ *www.timorne.com* ⇤ *14 rooms* ⑩ *Free Breakfast.*

Villa Marie Saint-Barth

$$$$ | HOTEL | Airy bungalows with views of the Bay of Flanders, some with private pools, paint a picture of understated luxury at this boutique hotel in Colombier. **Pros:** peaceful getaway; great service; good restaurant and spa. **Cons:** not on the beach; pricey, as with all St. Barth properties; farther from the action. $ *Rooms from: €700 ⊠ Colombier ☎ 0590/77–52–52 ⊕ en.saint-barth. villamarie.fr ⮌ 23 rooms ⑪ Free Breakfast.*

Corossol

Traces of the island's French provincial origins are evident in this two-street fishing village with a little rocky beach. Stop for the scenery on the way up to Anse de Colombier; it's a 10-minute drive from Gustavia.

Flamands

Beaches

Anse des Flamands

BEACH | This is the most beautiful of the hotel beaches—a roomy strip of silken sand. Come here for lunch and then spend the afternoon sunning, enjoying long beach walks, and swimming in the turquoise water. From the beach, you can take a brisk hike along a paved sidewalk to the top of the now-extinct volcano believed to have given birth to St. Barth. **Amenities:** food and drink; toilets. **Best for:** snorkeling; swimming; walking. ⊠ *Anse des Flamands.*

🍴 Restaurants

★ La Case de L'Isle

$$$$ | MODERN FRENCH | You can't top the view or the service at this waterfront restaurant at the renowned Cheval Blanc St-Barth Isle de France, and at night there is no more romantic spot on the island. Lighter versions of traditional French fare are served. **Known for:** toes-in-the-sand dining; romantic ambience; creative preparations. $ *Average main: €52 ⊠ Cheval Blanc St-Barth Isle de France, Flamands Beach, Anse des Flamands ☎ 0590/27–61– 81 ⊕ www.chevalblanc.com/en.*

La Langouste

$$$ | **FRENCH FUSION** | This small but friendly beachside restaurant in the pool courtyard of Hôtel Baie des Anges lives up to its name by serving fresh-grilled local lobster—and lobster thermidor—at prices that are somewhat gentler than at most other island venues. Try starters like crab and guacamole tiramisu, grilled scallops, or one of soups, including classic Caribbean fish soup and lobster bisque. **Known for:** lobster thermidor; classic French desserts; pick-your-own lobster from the tank. $ *Average main: €28 ⊠ Hôtel Baie des Anges, Anse des Flamands ☎ 0590/27–63–61 ⊕ www. hotel-baie-des-anges.com ☉ Closed Tues. and late Aug.–mid-Oct.*

Hotels

★ Cheval Blanc St-Barth Isle de France

$$$$ | **RESORT** | Nestled along a pristine white-sand beach, in tropical gardens, or on a hillside, the spacious suites and villas of this intimate, casual resort are private and luxurious. **Pros:** prime beach location; excellent restaurant; great spa. **Cons:** you may not want to leave; pricey, like everything on the island; car needed to get around. $ *Rooms from: €1625 ⊠ Baie des Flamands, Anse des Flamands ☎ 0590/27–61–81 ⊕ www.chevalblanc.com ☉ Closed late Aug.–late Oct. ⋈ 61 rooms ﾺ Free Breakfast.*

Hôtel Baie des Anges

$$ | **HOTEL** | **FAMILY** | Everyone is treated like family at this casual retreat with 10 clean, spacious units, two of which are modern two-bedroom oceanfront suites, one with a Jacuzzi. **Pros:** on St. Barth's longest beach; family-friendly; excellent value. **Cons:** not super fancy; the boutique is good but not likely to cover all your shopping needs; a bit remote from town, so you'll need a car. $ *Rooms from: €300 ⊠ Anse des Flamands ☎ 0590/27–63–61 ⊕ www.hotel-baie-des-anges.com ☉ Closed Sept. ⋈ 10 rooms ﾺ No Meals.*

Gouverneur

Beaches

Anse du Gouverneur

BEACH | **FAMILY** | Because it's so secluded, this beach continues to be a popular place for nude sunbathing. Truly beautiful, it has blissful swimming and views of St. Kitts, Saba, and St. Eustatius. Venture here at the end of the day and watch the sun set behind the hills. The road here from Gustavia also offers spectacular vistas. Legend has it that pirates' treasure is buried in the vicinity. There are no restaurants, toilets, or other services here, so plan accordingly. **Amenities:** parking (no fee). **Best for:** nudists; sunset; swimming; walking. ⊠ *Le Gouverneur*.

Grand Cul de Sac

Beaches

Anse de Grand Cul de Sac

BEACH | FAMILY | The shallow, reef-protected beach is nice for small children, fly-fishermen, kayakers, and windsurfers—and for the amusing frigate birds that dive-bomb the water fishing for their lunch. You needn't do your own fishing; you can have a wonderful lunch at one of the excellent restaurants nearby and use their lounge chairs for the afternoon. You may see some turtles in the shallow water. After storms the water may be a bit murky. **Amenities:** food and drink; parking (no fee); toilets; water sports. **Best for:** swimming; walking. ⊠ *Grand Cul de Sac*.

Restaurants

Beach House St. Barth

$$$ | MEDITERRANEAN | Rosewood Le Guanahani's open-air restaurant serves fresh Mediterranean-Caribbean fare, family-style. After lunch, sunbathe on the lounge deck with a cocktail. **Known for:** waterfront dining; Mediterranean bites; casual luxury. ⑤ *Average main: €30* ⊠ *Rosewood Le Guanahani, Grand Cul de Sac* ☎ *0590/52–90–01* ⊕ *www.rosewoodhotels.com*.

🛏 Hotels

Hotel Les Ondines Sur La Plage

$$$$ | APARTMENT | FAMILY | Right on the beach, this reasonably priced, intimate gem comprises modern, comfortable apartments with room to spread out. **Pros:** close to restaurants and water sports; nice pool; airport transfers included. **Cons:** narrow beach; you'll need a car; not a resort. ⑤ *Rooms from: €680* ⊠ *Grand Cul de Sac* ☎ *0590/27–69–64* ⊕ *www.st-barths.com/les-ondines* ⊙ *Closed Sept.–mid-Oct.* ⇆ *6 units* ⚭ *Free Breakfast*.

★ Le Barthélemy Hotel & Spa

$$$$ | **HOTEL** | **FAMILY** | Perched on a crescent bay, this beachfront hotel exudes Parisian chic with Caribbean flair. **Pros:** ultimate luxury; restaurants, rooftop bar, and spa on-site; spacious villas with kitchens and private pools. **Cons:** not budget-friendly; high levels of service may spoil you; service can be relaxed. $ *Rooms from: €1450* ✉ *Baie de Grand Cul de Sac, Grand Cul de Sac* ☎ *0590/77–48–48* ⊕ *www.lebarthelemyhotel.com/en* ⇒ *44 rooms* ❤ *Free Breakfast.*

★ Le Sereno

$$$$ | **RESORT** | Those seeking a restorative, sensuous escape discover nirvana at the quietly elegant, aptly named Le Sereno, set on a beachy cove of turquoise sea, between the island's highest mountain and the foamy waves. **Pros:** beach location; super-chic comfort; spa and restaurant on-site. **Cons:** pricey, as with most St. Barth properties; air-conditioning could be better in bathrooms; you won't want to go home. $ *Rooms from: €1300* ✉ *B.P. 19 Grand-Cul-de-Sac, Grand Cul de Sac* ☎ *0590/29–83–00* ⊕ *www. lesereno.com* ✆ *Closed late Aug.–mid-Oct.* ⇒ *42 units* ❤ *Free Breakfast.*

★ Rosewood Le Guanahani St. Barth

$$$$ | **RESORT** | **FAMILY** | The island's largest resort has luxurious suites, most with ocean views and 20 with private swimming pools, plus impeccable service. **Pros:** fantastic spa; beachside sports; has one of the island's few children's programs. **Cons:** pricey; steep walk to beach; lots of walking around property. $ *Rooms from: €1850* ✉ *Grand Cul de Sac* ☎ *0590/52–90–00* ⊕ *www.rosewoodhotels.com* ✆ *Closed late Aug.–Oct.* ⇒ *66 rooms* ❤ *Free Breakfast* ☞ *Day passes available.*

Shopping

ART

Chez Pompi

ART GALLERIES | This is little more than a cottage whose first room is a gallery for the naive paintings of Pompi (Louis Ledée). You must call to make a reservation to visit. ✉ *Rte. de Toiny, Petit Cul de Sac* ☎ *0590/29–76–90.*

Grande Saline

 Beaches

★ Anse de Grande Saline

BEACH | With its peaceful seclusion and sandy ocean bottom, this is just about everyone's favorite beach and is great for swimming, too. Without any major development, it's an ideal Caribbean strand, though there can be a bit of wind at times. In spite of the prohibition, young and old alike go nude. The beach is a 10-minute walk up a rocky dune trail, so wear sneakers or water shoes, and bring a blanket, umbrella, and beach towels. There are several good lunch restaurants near the parking area, but the beach itself is just sand, sea, and sky. The big salt ponds here are no longer in use, and the place looks a little desolate on approach, but don't despair. **Amenities:** parking (no fee). **Best for:** nudists; swimming; walking. ⊠ *Grande Saline.*

 Restaurants

★ L' Esprit

$$$$ | **MODERN FRENCH** | **FAMILY** | Renowned chef Jean-Claude Dufour (formerly of Eden Rock) brings innovative dishes to a romantic terrace close to Saline Beach. The menu has lots of variety, from light French dishes with a Provençal twist to interesting salads that have included soba noodles with shrimp and lime to dishes such as roasted pigeon with foie gras, steak, and vegetarian options. **Known for:** outstanding service; excellent wine list; creative menu items. $ *Average main: €41* ⊠ *Anse de Grande Saline, Grande Saline* ☎ *0590/52–46–10* ⊘ *Closed Sun. and Mon. No lunch.*

Restaurant La Santa Fé

$$$$ | **FRENCH** | **FAMILY** | Perched at the top of the Lurin hills on the way to Gouverneur Beach, this relaxed and scenic restaurant serves panoramic views with both lunch and dinner. The chef comes from Provence and trained at some of its best restaurants before moving to the Caribbean. **Known for:** beautiful presentation; generous portions; incredible views of neighboring islands. $ *Average main: €42* ⊠ *Rte. de Lurin, Lurin* ☎ *0590/27–61–04* ⊘ *Closed Tues., Wed., and late June-Sept.*

★ Tamarin St Barth

$$$$ | **INTERNATIONAL** | With a beautiful tropical garden that shades the lounge chairs surrounding the palapa of the restaurant, Tamarin is tops for dinner near Grande Saline Beach. The service is attentive and friendly, and the wine list is excellent. **Known for:** variety of entrées; great service; superb outdoor dining. $ *Average main: €45* ⊠ *Grande Saline, Grande Saline* ☎ *0590/29–27–74* ⊕ *www.tamarinstbarth.com* ⊗ *Closed Mon.*

 ## Hotels

Salines Garden Cottages

$ | HOUSE | FAMILY | Budget-conscious beach lovers who don't require a lot of coddling need look no further than these petite garden cottages, a short stroll from St. Barth's best beach. **Pros:** only property walkable to Grande Saline Beach; quiet; good restaurants nearby. **Cons:** not very private; strict cancellation policy; far from town. $ *Rooms from: €250* ⊠ *Grande Saline* ☎ *0590/41–94–29* ⊕ *www.salinesgarden.com* ⊅ *5 cottages* ⫟ *Free Breakfast.*

Lorient

 ## Beaches

Anse de Lorient

BEACH | FAMILY | This beach is popular with families and surfers, who like its waves and central location. Be aware of the level of the tide, which can come in very quickly. Hikers and avid surfers like the walk over the hill to Pointe Milou in the late afternoon, when the waves roll in. **Amenities:** parking (no fee). **Best for:** snorkeling; surfing; swimming. ⊠ *Lorient.*

 ## Hotels

Les Mouettes

$ | HOUSE | FAMILY | This guesthouse offers clean, simply furnished, and economical bungalows with kitchenettes that open directly onto the beach but are also very close to the road. **Pros:** on the beach; family-friendly; less expensive than many St. Barth options. **Cons:** strict prepayment and cancellation policies; no pool, but you're on the beach; basic rooms without TVs. $ *Rooms from: €270* ⊠ *Lorient* ☎ *0590/27–77–91* ⊕ *www.lesmouetteshotel.com* ⊅ *7 bungalows* ⫟ *No Meals.*

St. Barth's Spas

Visitors to St. Barth can enjoy more than the comforts of home by taking advantage of the myriad wellness, spa, and beauty treatments available on the island. Major hotels—the Cheval Blanc St-Barth Isle de France and Christopher among them—have beautiful, comprehensive, on-site spas. Others, including Le Village St. Barth Hotel, Le Sereno (with its waterfront treatment pavillion), and Hôtel Le Toiny, have added spa cottages, where treatments and services can be arranged on-site. Depending on availability, all island visitors can book services at these locations. There's a new wellness retreat here, with metabolic and detox programs available. In addition, scores of independent therapists will come to your hotel room or villa and provide any therapeutic discipline you can think of, including yoga, Thai massage, shiatsu, reflexology, and even manicures, pedicures, and hairdressing. You can get recommendations at the tourist office in Gustavia.

🛍 Shopping

COSMETICS

Ligne St. Barth

OTHER HEALTH & BEAUTY | Superb skin-care products are made on-site from local tropical plants. ⊠ *Rte. de Saline, Lorient* ☎ *0590/27–82–63* ⊕ *www.lignestbarth.com*.

FOODSTUFFS

Bacchus

WINE/SPIRITS | Fine wines and gourmet delicacies, teas, and Nespresso coffee can be found here, an outpost of the St. Martin distributor. ⊠ *Place des Marais, Lorient* ☎ *0590/29–19–22* ⊕ *www.bacchussxm.com*.

JoJo Supermarché

SUPERMARKET | This well-stocked counterpart to Gustavia's supermarket gets daily deliveries of bread and produce. JoJoBurger, next door, is the local surfers' spot for a (very good) quick burger. ⊠ *Lorient* ☎ *0590/27–63–53*.

The secluded beach at Eden Rock is a sunbather's dream.

Pointe Milou

 Restaurants

★ Le Ti St Barth Caribbean Tavern

$$$$ | **ECLECTIC** | Owner Carole Gruson captures the island's wild spirit in her popular hilltop spot. Come to dance to great music with the attractive bar crowd, lounge at a pillow-strewn banquette, or chat on the torch-lighted terrace. **Known for:** lively crowd; legendary barbecue; fun nights from beginning to end. ⑤ *Average main: €66* ⊠ *Pointe Milou* ☎ *0590/27–97–71* ⊕ *www. tistbarth.com.*

 Hotels

★ Christopher

$$$$ | **RESORT** | **FAMILY** | This longtime favorite of European families delivers a high standard of professionalism and courteous service. **Pros:** comfortable elegance; family-friendly; good value. **Cons:** three-night minimum; there's a bit of walking to get around the complex; on the water but not on a beach. ⑤ *Rooms from: €1850* ⊠ *Pointe Milou* ☎ *0590/27–63–63* ⊕ *www.hotelchristopher. com* ☉ *Closed mid-Aug.–mid-Oct.* ⇨ *45 units* ⦁◎⦁ *Free Breakfast* ☞ *3-night minimum.*

St-Jean

There is a monument at the crest of the hill that divides St-Jean from Gustavia. Called *The Arawak,* it symbolizes the soul of St. Barth. A warrior, one of the earliest inhabitants of the area (AD 800–1,800) holds a lance in his right hand and stands on a rock shaped like the island; in his left hand he holds a conch shell, which sounds the cry of nature; perched beside him are a pelican (which symbolizes the air and survival by fishing) and an iguana (which represents the earth). The half-mile-long crescent of sand at St-Jean is the island's favorite beach. A popular activity is watching and photographing the hair-raising airplane landings (but it is *extremely* dangerous to stand at the beach end of the runway). Some of the best shopping on the island is here as are several restaurants.

Beaches

Baie de St-Jean
BEACH | FAMILY | Like a mini Côte d'Azur—beachside bistros, terrific shopping, bungalow hotels, bronzed sunbathers, windsurfing, and day-trippers who tend to arrive on *big* yachts—the reef-protected strip is divided by the Eden Rock promontory. Except when the hotels are filled, you can rent chaises and umbrellas at the Pearl Beach restaurant or Eden Rock, where you can lounge for hours over lunch. **Amenities:** food and drink; toilets. **Best for:** partiers; walking. ⊠ *St-Jean.*

Restaurants

★ Sand Bar Eden Rock
$$$$ | ECLECTIC | Eden Rock hotel is legendary; this laid-back beach restaurant is just one more reason to love it. Lunch time is lively but relaxed with a DJ pumping tunes by the sparkling sea, and there are many tempting gourmet pizzas on offer. **Known for:** music; black truffle fontina cheese pizza; fresh herbs from the hotel's garden. ⑤ *Average main: €52* ⊠ *Eden Rock, Baie de St-Jean, St-Jean* ☎ *0590/29–81–86* ⊕ *www.oetkercollection.com.*

🛏 Hotels

★ Eden Rock St Barths
$$$$ | RESORT | FAMILY | Even on an island known for gourmet cuisine and luxury hotels, this iconic luxury hotel stands out thanks to top-tier Jean-Georges Vongerichten eateries, spacious rooms,

stunning bay views, and cosseting service. **Pros:** chic clientele; beach setting; stylish facilities. **Cons:** some construction or site work may continue for a bit; car needed to tour the entire island; some suites near street are noisy. ⑤ *Rooms from: €900 ⊠ Baie de St-Jean, St-Jean* ☎ *0590/29–79–99, 877/992–0070 in U.S.* ⊕ *www.oetkercollection.com* ⊙ *Closed late Aug.–Nov. 1* 🛏 *37 units* ⦿ *Free Breakfast.*

★ Hotel Manapany

$$$$ | **RESORT** | On a private beach of Anse des Cayes, this breezy yet luxurious B Signature resort (the first outside of mainland France) is an ecofriendly paradise, with solar panels and electric cars on property. **Pros:** five minutes to the airport with complimentary transfers; spa faces the sea; open-air restaurant. **Cons:** not in the action of Baie St-Jean; pricey; like everything here; you may be spoiled by high levels of service. ⑤ *Rooms from: €1030 ⊠ Anse de Cayes, St-Jean* ☎ *0590/27-66-55* ⊕ *hotelmanapany-stbarth.com* 🛏 *43 units* ⦿ *Free Breakfast.*

★ Le Village St. Barth Hotel

$$ | **HOTEL** | **FAMILY** | For two generations the Charneau family has offered friendly hotel service, villa advantages, and reasonable rates, making guests feel like a part of the family. **Pros:** convenient location near beach and town; wonderful management; on-site spa and gym. **Cons:** not in the center of the action; rooms close to street can be noisy; steep walk to hotel, many steps. ⑤ *Rooms from: €295 ⊠ Colline de St-Jean, St-Jean* ☎ *0590/27–61–39, 800/651–8366 in U.S.* ⊕ *www.levillagestbarth.com* 🛏 *25 units* ⦿ *Free Breakfast.*

Les Îlets de la Plage

$$$$ | **B&B/INN** | **FAMILY** | On the far side of the airport and the far corner of Baie de St-Jean, these well-priced, island-style one-, two-, and three-bedroom bungalows are nestled either on the beach itself or among lush tropical gardens on the hillside, with stunning views of the Bay. The units have small kitchens, open-air sitting areas, and comfortable bathrooms. **Pros:** beach location; apartment conveniences; front porches. **Cons:** limited air-conditioning; near airport, so you will hear some small planes taking off; only small pets allowed. ⑤ *Rooms from: €550 ⊠ Plage de St-Jean, St-Jean* ☎ *0590/27–88–57* ⊕ *www.lesilets.com* ⊙ *Closed Sept. 1-Oct. 15* 🛏 *12 units* ⦿ *Free Breakfast.*

Pearl Beach Saint Barth

$$$$ | **HOTEL** | This chic but casual boutique property on busy St-Jean beach is fun for social types; the nonstop house party may well spill onto the terraces and last into the wee hours. **Pros:**

party central at beach, restaurant, and pool; in town; many places of interest are walking distance away. **Cons:** some noise from the airport; you'll need a car to get to other beaches; trendy social scene is not for everybody, especially light sleepers. ⑤ *Rooms from: €635 ⊠ Plage de St-Jean, St-Jean* ☎ *0590/52–81–20* ⊕ *pearlbeachstbarth.com* ⇨ *14 rooms* ⑩ *Free Breakfast.*

Villa Les Lataniers

$$$$ | B&B/INN | With breathtaking views of the ocean and St. Barth's famous red tile roofs plus personalized service, this hillside villa is the ultimate private getaway. **Pros:** infinity pool with sweeping views; 24/7 concierge service; private, comfortable luxury. **Cons:** need a car if you want to venture beyond St. Jean; pricey; since this is a private villa, you lose the convenience of resort life (like restaurant and spa on-site). ⑤ *Rooms from: €6000 ⊠ Wimco Villas, St-Jean* ☎ *800/932–3222* ⊕ *wimco.com* ⇨ *1 private villa* ⑩ *Free Breakfast* ⌁ *Price is per week.*

Nightlife

Le Nikki Beach

BARS | This place rocks on weekends at lunch—especially Sunday—when the scantily clad young and beautiful lounge on the white canvas banquettes. ⊠ *St-Jean* ☎ *0590/27–64–64* ⊕ *www. nikkibeach.com.*

Shopping

CLOTHING

Bamboo St Barth

MIXED CLOTHING | Beach fashions like cotton tunics, cocktails-on-the-yacht dresses, and sexy Australian swimsuits by Nicole Olivier and Seafolly can be paired with sassy sandals and costume jewelry. ⊠ *Pelican Beach, St-Jean* ☎ *0590/52–08–82* ⊕ *www.facebook. com/bamboo.stbarth.*

Black Swan

MIXED CLOTHING | This shop has an unparalleled selection of bathing suits, and it also offers beach dresses, hats, caps, and sunglasses. ⊠ *La Villa Créole, St-Jean* ☎ *0590/87–44–60* ⊕ *facebook.com/ blackswanstbarth.*

Cabane Saint-Barth

MIXED CLOTHING | Stocked with stenciled cotton, gauzy beach tops, great straw fedoras, caftans (for all ages), plus beachy shoes and accessories, this shop is open nonstop every day. ⊠ *Pélican, St-Jean* ☎ *0590/51–21–02* ⊕ *facebook.com/cabanesaintbarth.*

Filles des Iles

MIXED CLOTHING | In addition to high-quality, flattering French attire and sophisticated swimwear for all ages, this shop stocks delicious artisanal fragrances and chic accessories, like beautiful sandals. ⊠ *8 Villa Créole, St-Jean* ☏ *0590/29–04–08.*

Iléna St Barth

MIXED CLOTHING | Incredible beachwear and lingerie by Papueen, Sarda, and others includes Swarovski crystal–encrusted bikinis for the trendy set. ⊠ *La Villa Créole, St-Jean* ☏ *0590/29–84–05* ⊕ *www.facebook.com/Ilena.StBarth.*

KiWi Saint-Tropez

MIXED CLOTHING | This popular boutique for adults and kids has beach and resort wear for everyone, as well as a variety of beach bags and towels. ⊠ *3 Villa Créole, St-Jean* ☏ *0590/27–57–08* ⊕ *www.kiwi.fr.*

Lili Belle

MIXED CLOTHING | Their great selection includes chic, French designer beachwear and resort clothing. ⊠ *Pelican Plage, St-Jean* ☏ *0590/87–46–14.*

Morgan

MIXED CLOTHING | There's a great selection of trendy feminine clothing, accessories, shoes, hats, bags, and more at Morgan. ⊠ *La Villa Créole, St-Jean* ☏ *0590/27–57–22.*

SUD SUD St Barth

HANDBAGS | This store stocks bags, beachy shell jewelry, as well as gauzy cover-ups. ⊠ *La Villa Creole, St-Jean* ☏ *0590/27-98-75* ⊕ *https://www.facebook.com/Sud-Sud-St-Barth-1519235571710326/.*

FOODSTUFFS

Eden to Go

FOOD | This is the place to go for prepared picnics, meals, salads, and more. The emphasis is on freshness, so menu items change according to season and availability. This is not your average "boxed lunch" place; you could well get shrimp rolls on home-made bread, custom picnic baskets, or pork burgers. ⊠ *Les Galeries du Commerce, St-Jean* ☏ *0590/29–83–70* ⊕ *edentogo. com.*

Super U

FOOD | This modern, fully stocked supermarket across from the airport has a wide selection of French cheeses, pâtés, cured meats, produce, fresh bread, wine, and liquor. There is also a good selection of prepared foods and organic items. ⊠ *Face à l'aéroport, St-Jean* ☎ *0590/27–68–16* ⊙ *Closed Sun.*

HANDICRAFTS

Couleurs Provence

HOUSEWARES | This store stocks beautiful, handcrafted, French-made items like jacquard table linens in brilliant colors; decorative tableware, including trays in which dried flowers and herbs are suspended; and the island home fragrance line by L'Occitane. ⊠ *Rte. de Saline, St-Jean* ☎ *0590/52–48–51* ⊕ *www.facebook. com/CouleursProvence.*

HOME FURNISHINGS

French Indioc Design

HOUSEWARES | This beautiful shop is the brainchild of Karine Bruneel, a St. Barth–based architect and interior designer. There are lovely items to accent your home (or yacht) including furniture, textiles, glassware, and unusual decorative baskets, candles, and pottery. ⊠ *Centre Les Amandiers, St-Jean* ☎ *0590/29–66–38* ⊕ *www.frenchindiesdesign.fr.*

Activities

Boating and Sailing

St. Barth is a popular yachting and sailing center, thanks to its location midway between Antigua and St. Thomas.

Gustavia's harbor, 13 to 16 feet deep, has mooring and docking facilities for 40 yachts. There are also good anchorages at Public, Corossol, and Colombier. You can charter sailing and motorboats in Gustavia Harbor for as little as a half day, staffed or bareboat. Ask at the Gustavia tourist office or your hotel for a list of recommended charter companies.

Carib Waterplay

WINDSURFING | On St. Jean beach for over 35 years, this outfit lets you try windsurfing, kayaking, surfing, and stand-up paddling; rents waterbikes; and offers lessons for all ages. ⊠ *St-Jean* ☎ *0665/95–43–52* ⊕ *www.caribwaterplay.com.*

Jicky Marine Service

BOATING | This company offers private full-day outings on motor-boats, Zodiacs, and 47-foot catamarans to the uninhabited Île Fourchue for swimming, snorkeling, cocktails, or lunch, as well as scheduled cruises including weekly half- and full-day group cruises and twice-weekly group sunset catamaran cruises. Private fishing charters are also offered, as is private transport from St. Martin. Skippered motorboat rentals run about €1,400 per day. A one-hour group Jet Ski tour of the island is also offered, as are private tours. ⊠ *33 rue Jeanne D'Arc, Gustavia* ☎ *0590/27–70–34* ⊕ *www.jickymarine.com.*

St Barth Sailing

SAILING | Captain Eric offers his 47' sailing catamaran *Okeanos* for day trips for up to 16 people and charters for up to six. Half-day, full-day, and sunset Champagne cruises are available with all the amenities you could ask for either standard or available, or you can charter the boat and sail to the British Virgin Islands, Antigua and Barbuda, or St. Martin and Anguila, all available as seven-day, six-night sailing adventures. ☎ *690/19–00–15* ⊕ *www.saintbarth-sailing.com.*

St Barth Sailor

SAILING | Want to rent a bareboat or crewed catamaran and take off for your own tour of several islands? Captain Miguel Danet enables you to do exactly that, for a full-day, half-day, or sunset cruise. Extras are available, from special dining choices aboard to massage to scuba to underwater scooters. ☎ *690/18–60–66* ⊕ *www.stbarthsailor.com.*

Top Loc Boat Rental

BOATING | Charter a catamaran for a day of fun on the water. Rental for a half-day on the catamaran including an open bar is €750. Other rates/itineraries available. ⊠ *Airport Office, St-Jean* ☎ *0590/29–02–02* ⊕ *www.top-loc.com.*

Diving and Snorkeling

Several dive shops arrange scuba excursions. Depending on weather conditions, you may dive at **Pain de Sucre, Coco Island,** or toward nearby **Saba.** There's also an underwater shipwreck, plus sharks, rays, sea tortoises, coral, and the usual varieties of colorful fish. The waters on the island's leeward side are the calmest. For the uncertified, there's a shallow reef right off the beach at Anse des Cayes, which you can explore with mask and fins, and a hike down to the beach at Corossol brings you to a very popular snorkeling spot.

Ouanalao Dive

DIVING & SNORKELING | This well-regarded company offers PADI and CMAS, night dives, private dives and snorkeling, rental of fins, mask and snorkel, and more. Organized dives, a good dive shop, and instruction are offered at the Grand Cul-de Sac beach location. A two-tank dive is €170. A two-hour snorkeling trip to a nearby island starts at €70 per person. ⊠ *Grand Cul de Sac* ☎ *0690/63–74–34* ⊕ *www.ouanalaodive.com.*

Plongée Caraïbes

DIVING & SNORKELING | **FAMILY** | Recommended for its up-to-the-minute equipment, dive boat, and scuba discovery program, this company offers nitrox diving and certification. They also run two-hour group snorkeling trips on the *Blue Cat Catamaran* (€75 per person), or you can enjoy a private charter from €590. ⊠ *Quai de la République, Gustavia* ☎ *0590/27–55–94* ⊕ *www.sbhonline.com/activities/scuba/plongee-caraibes/.*

Réserve Naturelle de Saint-Barthélemy

SCUBA DIVING | Most of the waters surrounding St. Barth are protected in the island's nature reserve, which provides information from its Gustavia office. The diving here isn't nearly as rich as in more dive-centered destinations like Saba and St. Eustatius (Statia), but the options aren't bad either. ⊠ *Gustavia* ☎ *0590/27–88–18* ⊕ *www.reserves-naturelles.org/saint-barthelemy.*

Splash

SCUBA DIVING | This company offers PADI and CMAS (Confédération Mondiale des Activités Subaquatiques—World Underwater Federation) diver training at all levels. Instructors speak French and English. The boat leaves several times during the day and in the evening for a night dive; times are adjusted to suit preferences. SEABOB scuba scooters are available at reasonable rates. ⊠ *Gustavia* ☎ *0590/56–90–24.*

Fishing

Most fishing is done in the waters north of Lorient, Flamands, and Corossol. Popular catches are tuna, marlin, wahoo, and barracuda. The annual St. Barth Open Fishing Tournament is in mid-July.

Guided Tours

You can arrange island tours by minibus or car at hotel desks or through taxi operators in Gustavia or at the airport. The tourist office runs a variety of tours for about €50 for a half day for up to eight people. You can also download up-to-the-minute walking and driving tour itineraries from the office's website.

Hélène Bernier

GUIDED TOURS | St. Barth native Hélène gives complete island tours. Her family has lived on the island since the 17th century; she is also president of Barth Essential, a nonprofit organization she started to focus on preservation and environmental protection. ☎ *0690/63–46–09.*

JC Taxi

DRIVING TOURS | Since 1986, native-born Jean-Claude has been providing safe and comfortable transportation in a 9-passenger van with executive seats. Island tours and night driving are available. ✉ *Gustavia* ☎ *0690/31–59–00 (WhatsApp).*

St. Barth Mobilité

SPECIAL-INTEREST TOURS | This company offers transportation, tours, and guided help for those with limited mobility. ☎ *0690/77–66–73* ⊕ *www.stbarthmobilite.com.*

ANGUILLA

Updated by
Riselle Celestina

👁 Sights   🍴 Restaurants   🛏 Hotels   🛍 Shopping   🍸 Nightlife

★★★★☆   ★★★★☆   ★★★★☆   ★★★☆☆   ★★★☆☆

WELCOME TO ANGUILLA

TOP REASONS TO GO

★ **Beautiful Beaches:** Miles of brilliant beach ensure you have a high-quality spot on which to lounge.

★ **Great Restaurants:** The dining scene offers both fine dining and delicious casual food on and off the beach.

★ **Fun, Low-Key Nightlife:** A funky late-night local music scene features reggae and string bands.

★ **Upscale Accommodations:** Excellent luxury resorts coddle you in comfort.

★ **Hidden Bargains:** You'll find a few relative bargains for both food and lodging if you look hard enough.

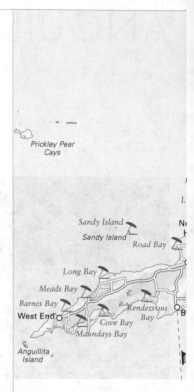

Prickley Pear Cays

Sandy Island
Sandy Island
Road Bay

Long Bay
Meads Bay
Barnes Bay
West End
Cove Bay
Maundays Bay

Rendezvous Bay

Anguillita Island

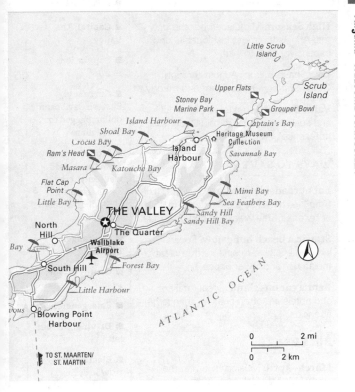

Little Scrub
Island

Upper Flats

Scrub
Island

Stoney Bay
Marine Park

Grouper Bowl

Island Harbour

Captain's Bay

Heritage Museum
Collection

Shoal Bay

Crocus Bay

Island
Harbour

Savannah Bay

Ram's Head

Masara

Katoucha Bay

Flat Cap
Point

Mimi Bay

Little Bay

Sea Feathers Bay

THE VALLEY

Sandy Hill
Sandy Hill Bay

North
Hill

The Quarter

Wallblake
Airport

Bay

South Hill

Forest Bay

Little Harbour

ATLANTIC OCEAN

Blowing Point
Harbour

vous

0   2 mi

0   2 km

TO ST. MAARTEN/
ST. MARTIN

ISLAND SNAPSHOT

WHEN TO GO

High Season: Mid-December through mid-April is the most fashionable (and expensive) time to visit.

Low Season: From August through October, the weather is hot and muggy.

Value Season: From late April to July and again November to mid-December, hotel prices drop 20% to 50%.

WAYS TO SAVE

Eat at roadside vendors. Head to "The Strip" in The Valley for local food trucks, or try one of the weekend pop-up BBQs.

Stay in a beach bungalow. Several local hotels have retained a true West Indian flair and lower prices.

Rent a car on-island. Local retailers and hotels are often cheaper than larger agencies.

BIG EVENTS

March–April: Musicians jam at the annual Moonsplash festival. ⊕ www.bankiebanx.net/moonsplash. Celebrate Anguilla culture during the Festival del Mar. ⊕ www.ivisitanguilla.com

May: Join literary aficionados at the Anguilla Lit Fest. ⊕ www.ivisitanguilla.com. The national love for boat racing peaks at the annual Anguilla Regatta. ⊕ www.anguilla-regatta.com

July–August: Anguilla Summer Fest features two weeks of pageants, parades, and fireworks.

AT A GLANCE

■ **Capital:** The Valley

■ **Population:** 15,279

■ **Currency:** Eastern Caribbean dollar; pegged to U.S. dollar

■ **Money:** Some ATMs are closed weekends; credit cards accepted; U.S. dollar widely accepted

■ **Language:** English

■ **Country Code:** 1 264

■ **Emergencies:** 911

■ **Driving:** On the left

■ **Electricity:** 110v/60 cycles; plugs are U.S. standard two-prong

■ **Time:** Same as New York during daylight saving time; one hour ahead otherwise

■ **Documents:** A valid passport and must have a return or ongoing ticket

Peace, pampering, great food, and a wonderful local music scene are among the star attractions on Anguilla (pronounced an- *gwill*-a). Beach lovers may become giddy when they first spot the island from the air; its blindingly white sand and lustrous blue-and-aquamarine waters are mesmerizing. And if you like sophisticated cuisine served in casually elegant open-air settings, this may well become your culinary Shangri-la.

The island's name, a reflection of its shape, is most likely a derivative of *anguille,* which is French for "eel." (French explorer Pierre Laudonniere is credited with having given the island this name when he sailed past it in 1556.) In 1631 the Dutch built a fort here, but so far no one has been able to locate its site. English settlers from St. Kitts colonized the island in 1650, with plans to cultivate tobacco and, later, cotton and then sugar. But the thin soil and scarce water doomed these enterprises. Except for a brief period of independence, when it broke from its association with St. Kitts and Nevis in the late 1960s, Anguilla has remained a British colony ever since.

From the early 1800s various island federations were formed and disbanded, with Anguilla all the while simmering over its subordinate status and forced union with St. Kitts. Anguillians twice petitioned for direct rule from Britain and twice were ignored. In 1967, when St. Kitts, Nevis, and Anguilla became an associated state, the mouse roared; citizens kicked out St. Kitts's policemen, held a self-rule referendum, and for two years conducted their own affairs. To what *Time* magazine called "a cascade of laughter around the world," a British "peacekeeping force" of 100 paratroopers from the Elite Red Devil unit parachuted onto the island, squelching Anguilla's designs for autonomy but helping a team of royal engineers stationed there to improve the port and build roads and schools. Today Anguilla elects a House of Assembly and its own leader to handle internal affairs, and a British governor is responsible for public service, the police, the judiciary, and external affairs. Some tourists may still be wondering whose responsibility it is to repair roads, some of which are absolute patchworks.

The territory of Anguilla includes a few islets (or cays, pronounced "keys"), such as Scrub Island, Dog Island, Prickly Pear Cay, Sandy Island, and Sombrero Island. The 15,000 or so island residents are predominantly of African descent, but there are also many of Irish background, whose ancestors came from St. Kitts in the 1600s. Historically, because the limestone land was unfit for agriculture, attempts at enslavement never lasted long; consequently, Anguilla doesn't bear the scars of slavery found on so many other Caribbean islands. Instead, Anguillians became experts at making a living from the sea and are known for their boatbuilding and fishing skills. Tourism is the stable economy's growth industry, but the government carefully regulates expansion to protect the island's natural resources and beauty. New hotels are relatively small, select, casino-free, and generally expensive; Anguilla emphasizes its high-quality service, serene surroundings, and friendly people.

Planning

Getting Here and Around

AIR

American Airlines' inaugural flight from Miami to Anguilla in 2021 marked the beginning of nonstop flights to Anguilla from the United States. American has two to three flights per week from Miami, depending on the time of year. You can also get here fast by flying to St. Maarten's Princess Juliana International SXM Airport and taking a nearby ferry to Anguilla, about a half-hour ride away. Air Sunshine also flies several times a day from St. Thomas and San Juan, Cape Air from St. Thomas once a week, and Anguilla Air Services flies from St. Maarten and St. Barth. Silver Airway flies in from San Juan. TransAnguilla provides scheduled flights throughout the Caribbean.

LOCAL AIRLINE CONTACTS Air Sunshine. ☎ 800/327–8900 ⊕ www.airsunshine.com. **Anguilla Air Services.** ☎ 264/498–5922 ⊕ www.anguillaairservices.com. **Tradewind Aviation.** ☎ 800/376–7922, 203/267–3305 ⊕ www.flytradewind.com. **TransAnguilla Airways.** ☎ 264/497–8690 ⊕ www.transanguilla.com.

AIRPORT Clayton J. Lloyd International Airport. ☎ 264/497–3510 ⊕ www.gov.ai/airport.php.

BOAT AND FERRY

Public ferries run frequently between Anguilla and Marigot on French St. Martin. Boats leave from Blowing Point on Anguilla three times daily (same from Marigot, St. Martin) between 7 am and 6 pm. You pay a $23 departure tax before boarding ($5 for day trippers coming through the Blowing Point terminal—but be sure to make this clear at the window where you pay), in addition to the $20 one-way fare. Fares require cash payment. Children under 12 years of age are $10. On very windy days the 20-minute trip can be fairly bouncy. The drive between the Marigot ferry terminal and the St. Maarten airport is vastly faster thanks to the causeway (bridge) across Simpson Bay lagoon. Transfers by speedboat to Anguilla are available from a terminal right at the airport at a cost of about $85 per person (arranged directly with a company or through your Anguilla hotel). Private ferry companies listed below run four or more round-trips a day, coinciding with major flights, between Blowing Point and Princess Juliana airport in Dutch St. Maarten. On the St. Maarten side they will bring you right to the terminal in a van, or you can just walk across the parking lot. These trips are $75 one-way or $130 round-trip (cash only) and usually include departure taxes. There are also private charters available.

CONTACTS Funtime Ferry. ☎ 264/497–6511 ⊕ www.funtimecharters.com. **Link Ferries.** ☎ 264/772–4901 ⊕ www.linkferry.com.

CAR

Although many of the rental cars on-island have the driver's side on the left as in North America, Anguillian roads are like those in the United Kingdom—driving is on the left side of the road. It's easy to get the hang of, but the roads can be rough, so be cautious, and observe the 30 mph (48 kph) speed limit. Roundabouts are probably the biggest driving obstacle for most. As you approach, give way to the vehicle on your right; once you're in the roundabout, you have the right of way.

Car Rentals: A temporary Anguilla driver's license is required to rent a car—you can get into real trouble if you're caught driving without one. You get it for $20 (good for three months) through any of the car-rental agencies at the time you pick up your car; you'll also need your valid driver's license from home. Rental rates start at about $45 to $55 per day, plus insurance.

CONTACTS Andy's Auto Rental. ✉ Blowing Point Village ☎ 264/584–7010, 264/235-7010 Whatsapp ⊕ www.andyrentals.com. **Avis.** ✉ Airport Rd. ☎ 264/497–2642 ⊕ www.avisanguilla.com. **Bryans Car Rental.** ✉ Blowing Point Village ☎ 203/992-5407 from the US,

264/497–6407 ⊕ *www.bryanscarrentals.com.* **Moke Anguilla.**
⊠ *Meads Bay, West End Village* ☎ *264/581-5000* ⊕ *www.mokean-guilla.com.*

TAXI

Taxis are fairly expensive, so if you plan to explore many beaches and restaurants, it may be more cost-effective to rent a car. Taxi rates are regulated by the government, and there are fixed fares from point to point, listed in brochures the drivers should have handy and published in local guides. It's about $22 from the airport or $28 from Blowing Point Ferry to West End hotels. Posted rates are for one or two people; each additional passenger adds $5, and there is a $1 charge for each piece of luggage beyond the allotted two. You can also hire a taxi for a flat rate of $28 an hour. A surcharge of $4 applies to trips between 6 pm and midnight. After midnight it's $10. You'll always find taxis at the Blowing Point Ferry landing and the airport at the taxi dispatch, but you'll need to call for hotel and restaurant pickups and arrange ahead with the driver who took you if you need a late-night return from a nightclub or bar.

Health and Safety

Dengue, chikungunya, and Zika have all been reported throughout the Caribbean at some time. Although there have been no cases in recent years, we recommend that you protect yourself from these mosquito-borne illnesses by keeping your skin covered and/or wearing mosquito repellent. The mosquitoes that transmit these viruses are as active by day as they are by night. Many locals swear by a product called "Mosquito Milk," a roll-on insect repellent available at many Caribbean pharmacies; it has a lemongrass fragrance mosquitoes seem to hate.

Hotels and Resorts

Anguilla is known for its luxurious resorts and villas, but there are also some places that mere mortals can afford (and a few that are downright bargains).

Resorts. Anguilla is known for luxurious, expensive resorts.

Villas and rentals. Private villa rentals are becoming more common and are improving in quality of design and upkeep every season as development on the island accelerates. Condos, with full kitchens and multiple bedrooms, are great for families or for longer stays.

Hotel reviews have been shortened. For full information, visit Fodors.com.

What It Costs in U.S. Dollars			
$	$$	$$$	$$$$
RESTAURANTS			
under $12	$12–$20	$21–$30	over $30
HOTELS			
under $275	$275–$375	$376–$475	over $475

Visitor Information

CONTACTS Anguilla Tourist Board. ✉ *Coronation Ave., The Valley* ☎ *264/497–2759* ⊕ *www.ivisitanguilla.com.*

 Sights

Exploring Anguilla is mostly about checking out the spectacular beaches and resorts. The island has only a few roads. Locals are happy to provide directions, but using the readily available tourist map is the best idea. Visit the Anguilla Tourist Board, centrally located on Coronation Avenue in The Valley.

You can take a free, self-guided tour of the Anguilla Heritage Trail, consisting of 10 important historical sights that can be explored independently in any order. Wallblake House, in The Valley, is the main information center for the trail, or you can just look for the large boulders with descriptive plaques.

Heritage Museum Collection

HISTORY MUSEUM | FAMILY | A remarkable opportunity to learn about Anguilla, this tiny museum (complete with gift shop) is painstakingly curated by Colville Petty. Old photographs and local records and artifacts trace the island's history over four millennia, from the days of the Arawaks. High points include historical documents of the Anguilla Revolution and photo albums chronicling island life, from devastating hurricanes to a visit from Queen Elizabeth in 1964. You can see examples of ancient pottery shards and stone tools along with fascinating photographs of the island in the early 20th century—many depicting the heaping and exporting of salt and the christening of schooners—and a complete set of beautiful postage stamps issued by Anguilla since 1967. ✉ *East End at Pond Ground* ☎ *264/235-7440* 💲 *$10* ⊗ *Closed Wed., Thu., Sat. and Sun.*

Sights

Bethel Methodist Church, **1**

Heritage Museum Collection, **5**

Island Harbour, **6**

Old Factory, **4**

Sandy Ground, **2**

Wallblake House, **3**

Restaurants

Blanchards, **7**

Blanchards Beach Shack, **8**

Cafe Celeste at Malliouhana, **9**

da'Vida, **19**

Dolce Vita Italian Beach Restaurant & Bar, **13**

Elvis' Beach Bar, **15**

English Rose Bar and Restaurant, **18**

Hibernia Restaurant and Art Gallery, **21**

Jacala Beach Restaurant, **10**

Madeariman Reef Bar and Restaurant, **20**

Mango's Seaside Grill, **4**

Ocean Echo, **5**

Picante, **3**

Roy's Bayside Grill, **12**

SandBar, **14**

Sharky's, **2**

Straw Hat, **6**

Tasty's, **16**

Tokyo Bay, **11**

Trattoria Tramonto and Oasis Beach Bar, **1**

Veya and Meze at Veya, **17**

Hotels

Allamanda Beach Club, **15**

Altamer, **1**

Anguilla Great House Beach Resort, **12**

Cap Juluca, **6**

Caribella Beach Resort, **2**

Carimar Beach Club, **8**

CuisinArt Golf Resort and Spa, **11**

Four Seasons Resort and Residences Anguilla, **5**

Frangipani Beach Resort, **3**

Malliouhana, An Auberge Resort, **9**

Meads Bay Beach Villas, **4**

Paradise Cove, **7**

Serenity Cottages, **16**

Shoal Bay Villas, **14**

Turtle's Nest Beach Resort, **10**

Zemi Beach House Hotel & Spa / Residences, **13**

Ram's Head

Masara

Flat Cap Point

Little Bay

North Hill

Crocus Bay

Sandy Island

Sandy Island

Road Bay

Sandy Ground Village

South Hill

Wallblake Airport

Long Bay

Long Bay Village

Little Harbour

Meads Bay

Barnes Bay

West End

Cove Bay

Rendezvous Bay

Blowing Point Harbour

Shoal Bay West

Maundays Bay

Anguillita Island

0   2 mi

0   2 km

TO ST. MAARTEN/ ST. MARTIN

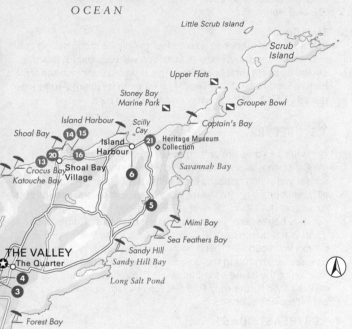

Anguilla

ATLANTIC OCEAN

Little Scrub Island

Scrub Island

Upper Flats

Stoney Bay Marine Park

Grouper Bowl

Captain's Bay

Island Harbour

Scilly Cay

Shoal Bay

14 **15**

21 Heritage Museum Collection

20

13

Island Harbour

Crocus Bay

16

6

Savannah Bay

Katouche Bay

Shoal Bay Village

5

Mimi Bay

Sea Feathers Bay

THE VALLEY

Sandy Hill

The Quarter

Sandy Hill Bay

4

Long Salt Pond

3

Forest Bay

ST. MARTIN

Ile Tintamarre

KEY	
1	*Exploring Sights*
1	*Restaurants*
1	*Hotels*
⛴	*Ferry*
⚐	*Beaches*
◪	*Dive Sights*

Island Harbour

MARINA/PIER | Anguillians have been fishing for centuries in the brightly painted, simple, handcrafted fishing boats that line the shore of the harbor. It's hard to believe, but skillful pilots take these little boats out to sea as far as 50 or 60 miles (80 or 100 km). Late afternoon is the best time to see the day's catch, and there are a couple of good, laid-back beach restaurants here. ⊠ *Island Harbor Rd.*

Sandy Ground

BEACH | Almost everyone who comes to Anguilla stops by this central beach, home to several popular open-air bars and restaurants, as well as boat-rental operations. This is where you catch the ferry for tiny Sandy Island, 2 miles (3 km) offshore for about $40 round-trip. ☎ *264/476–6534* ⊕ *www.mysandyisland.com.*

Beaches

Anguilla's beaches are among the best and most beautiful in the Caribbean. You can find long, deserted stretches suitable for sunset walks and beaches lined with lively bars and restaurants—all surrounded by crystal-clear warm waters in several shades of turquoise. The sea is calmest at 2½-mile-long (4-km-long) Rendezvous Bay, where gentle breezes tempt sailors. But Shoal Bay (East) is the quintessential Caribbean beach. The white sand is so soft and abundant that it pools around your ankles. Maundays Bay also ranks among the island's best beaches. Maundays is the location of the island's famous resort Cap Juluca. Meads Bay's arc is dominated by the tony Four Seasons Resort. Anguilla doesn't permit topless sunbathing.

NORTHEAST COAST

Captain's Bay

BEACH | On the north coast just before the eastern tip of the island, this quarter-mile stretch of perfect white sand is bounded by a rocky shoreline where Atlantic waves crash. If you make the tough, four-wheel-drive-only trip along the dirt road that leads to the northeastern end of the island toward Junk's Hole, you'll be rewarded with peaceful isolation. The surf here slaps the sands with a vengeance, and the undertow is strong—so wading is the safest water sport. **Amenities:** none. **Best for:** solitude.

Island Harbour

BEACH | For centuries Anguillians have ventured from these sands in colorful handmade fishing boats. Mostly calm waters are surrounded by a slender beach—good sightseeing, but not much for swimming or lounging. But there are a couple of good restaurants

(Hibernia, offering dinner, and Falcon Nest, a casual spot for lunch and dinner). **Amenities:** food and drink; toilets. **Best for:** partiers.

NORTHWEST COAST
Little Bay

BEACH | On the north coast, not far from The Valley, this small gray-sand beach is a favored spot for snorkeling and night dives. It's essentially accessible only by water, as it's backed by sheer cliffs lined with agave and creeping vines. The easiest way to get here is a five-minute boat ride from Crocus Bay (about $10 round-trip). There are no amenities, so take some snacks with you. The only way to access the beach from the road is to clamber down the cliffs by rope to explore the caves and surrounding reef—for young, agile, and experienced climbers only. Do not leave personal items in cars parked here, because theft can be a problem. **Amenities:** none. **Best for:** snorkeling.

Road Bay (*Sandy Ground*)

BEACH | The big pier here is where the cargo ships dock, but so do some impressive yachts, sailboats, and fishing boats. The brown-sugar sand is home to terrific restaurants that hop from day through dawn, including Roy's Bayside Grill, Johnno's, and Elvis', the quintessential (and rather famous) beach bar. This beach is where the famous "August Monday" annual beach party takes place. There are all kinds of boat charters available here. The snorkeling isn't very good, but the sunset vistas are glorious, especially with a rum punch in your hand. **Amenities:** food and drink. **Best for:** sunset.

Sandy Island

BEACH | A popular day trip, tiny Sandy Island shelters a pretty lagoon nestled in coral reefs about 2 miles (3 km) from Road Bay/Sandy Ground, with a restaurant that serves lunch and great islandy cocktails. From November through August you can take the shuttle from Sandy Ground ($40 round-trip). There is mooring for yachts and larger sailboats. Small boats can come right in the channel. ■ TIP➔ **The reef is great for snorkeling. Amenities:** food and drink. **Best for:** partiers; snorkeling; swimming. ⊕ *www. mysandyisland.com.*

★ Shoal Bay

BEACH | FAMILY | Anchored by seagrape and coconut trees, the 2-mile (3-km) powdered-sugar strand at Shoal Bay (not to be confused with Shoal Bay West, at the other end of the island) is one of the world's prettiest beaches. You can park free at any of the restaurants, including Tropical Sunset or Gwen's Reggae Bar & Grill, most of which either rent or provide chairs and umbrellas for patrons for about $20 a day per person (some offer chairs and umbrellas free of charge with lunch). There is plenty of room to stretch out in relative privacy, or you can bar-hop. The relatively broad beach has shallow water that is usually gentle, making this a great family beach; a coral reef not far from the shore is a wonderful snorkeling spot. Sunsets over the water are spectacular. **Amenities:** food and drink. **Best for:** sunset; swimming; walking.

SOUTHEAST COAST
Sandy Hill

BEACH | You can park anywhere along the dirt road to Sea Feathers Bay to visit this popular fishing center. What's good for the fishermen is also good for snorkelers, with a coral reef right near the shore. The beach here is not much of a lounging spot, but it's a favorite spot for local families to picnic. For those with creative culinary skills, it's a great place to buy lobsters and fish fresh from local waters in the afternoon. **Amenities:** food and drink. **Best for:** snorkeling; walking.

SOUTHWEST COAST
★ Maundays Bay

BEACH | The dazzling, platinum-white mile-long beach is especially great for swimming and long beach walks. It's no wonder that the Belmond Cap Juluca, one of Anguilla's premier resorts, chose this as its location. Public parking is straight ahead at the end of the road near Cap Juluca's Pimms restaurant. You can have lunch or dinner here (be prepared for the cost) or, depending on the season, book a massage in one of the beachside tents. **Amenities:** food and drink; parking (no fee); toilets. **Best for:** sunbathing; swimming; walking.

★ Meads Bay

BEACH | FAMILY | Arguably Anguilla's premier beach, Meads Bay is home to many of the island's top resorts (Malliouhana, Four Seasons) and a dozen fine restaurants. The powder-soft Champagne sand is great for a long walk and is as beautiful now as it has ever been. Park at any of the restaurants, and plan for lunch. Several of the restaurants offer chaises for patrons. **Amenities:** food and drink; parking (no fee); toilets. **Best for:** sunbathing; swimming; walking.

Rendezvous Bay

BEACH | FAMILY | Follow the signs to Anguilla Great House for public parking at this broad swath of pearl-white sand that is some 1½ miles (2½ km) long. The beach is lapped by calm, bluer-than-blue water and a postcard-worthy view of St. Martin. The expansive crescent is home to three resorts; stop in for a drink or a meal at one, or rent a chair and umbrella at one of the kiosks.

Meads Bay is home to powder-soft sand and many of the island's top resorts.

Don't miss the daylong party at the Dune Preserve, where Bankie Banx, Anguilla's most famous musician, presides. (Jimmy Buffett recorded a concert there several years back, too.) **Amenities:** food and drink; parking (no fee); toilets. **Best for:** sunbathing; swimming; walking.

Shoal Bay West

BEACH | This glittering bay bordered by mangroves and seagrapes is a lovely place to spend the day. The 1-mile-long (1½-km-long) beach offers sublime tranquility with coral reefs for snorkeling not too far from shore. Punctuate your day with lunch or dinner at beachside Trattoria Tramonto and you can use their chairs and umbrellas. Reach the beach by taking the main road to the West End and bearing left at the fork, then continuing to the end. Note that similarly named Shoal Bay is a separate beach on a different part of the island. **Amenities:** food and drink; parking (no fee); toilets. **Best for:** solitude; swimming; walking.

 Restaurants

Despite its small size, Anguilla has more than 70 restaurants: stylish temples of haute cuisine; classic, barefoot beachfront grills; roadside barbecue stands; food vans; and casual cafés. Many have breeze-swept terraces for dining under the stars. Call ahead—in winter to make a reservation and in late summer and fall to confirm whether the place is open. Anguillian restaurant meals are leisurely events, and service often has a relaxed pace, so settle in and enjoy. Most restaurant owners are actively and conspicuously present, especially at dinner.

★ Blanchards

$$$$ | ECLECTIC | Creative cuisine, an upscale atmosphere, attentive service, and an excellent wine cellar please the star-studded crowd at Blanchards, one of the best restaurants in the Caribbean. Ever changing but always good, the contemporary menu, with items such as the warm Brussels sprout Caesar and the sesame-crusted sea bass, wins over even the most sophisticated palates. **Known for:** exquisite presentation; fine dining; the owners' book *A Trip To The Beach* which has motivated many to visit. ⑤ *Average main: $38* ✉ *Meads Bay Beach, Long Bay Village* ☎ *264/497–6100* ⊕ *www.blanchardsrestaurant.com* ☉ *Closed Sun. No lunch. Closed end of Aug. to mid.–Oct.*

Blanchards Beach Shack

$$ | AMERICAN | FAMILY | This spin-off on the sands of Meads Bay Beach is the perfect antidote to high restaurant prices. Right next to Blanchards, this chartreuse-and-turquoise cottage serves delicious lunches and dinners of mahimahi BLT, all-natural burgers, tacos, and terrific salads and sandwiches, and there are lots of choices for children and vegetarians. **Known for:** generous portions; "the wait" from 12:30 on; beach food with a twist. ⑤ *Average main: $13* ✉ *Meads Bay Beach, Long Bay Village* ☎ *264/498–6100* ⊕ *www.blanchardsrestaurant.com* ☉ *Closed Sun. and end of Aug. to mid Oct.*

★ Cafe Celeste at Malliouhana

$$$$ | ECLECTIC | The romantic open-air setting of Cafe Celeste on a promontory overlooking Meads Bay sets the stage for a memorable meal. The café's dishes are inspired by Mediterranean seafaring cultures, including seafood spaghettini or conch tiradito made with soursop, peppers, scallions, and lime. **Known for:** grilled crayfish with lemon butter; the stunning view; Malli sunset cocktails. ⑤ *Average main: $36* ✉ *Meads Bay Beach, Long Bay Village* ☎ *264/497–6111* ⊕ *aubergeresorts.com/malliouhana/dine/celeste* ▭ *No credit cards* ☉ *Closed late Aug. to Oct.*

Da'Vida

$$$$ | ASIAN FUSION | FAMILY | Dining at this locally owned, fine dining restaurant on the pristine beach at Crocus Bay is a delight. A semi-open design allows the sounds and smells of the ocean to tantalize your senses while you dine on exquisite Asian-Mediterranean fusion dishes like mushroom and kale risotto and pan-seared miso grouper with lemongrass beurre blanc. **Known for:** tapas and cocktails at the Tamarind Lounge; friendly service; beachside sophistication. $ *Average main: $36* ✉ *Crocus Bay* ☎ *264/498–5433* ⊕ *www.davidaanguilla.com* ⊘ *Closed Mon. and Tues. and from Aug.–Nov.*

Dolce Vita Italian Beach Restaurant & Bar

$$$$ | **ITALIAN** | **FAMILY** | Serious Italian cuisine and warm and attentive service are provided in a romantic beachside pavilion in Sandy Ground. It all starts with meticulously sourced seafood and freshly made pasta, which stars in classic lasagna, linguine with clams, seafood risotto, and a meatless eggplant parmigiana. **Known for:** Italian wine selection; beachside dining; fresh catch of the day. $ *Average main: $43* ✉ *Sandy Ground, Sandy Ground Village* ☎ *264/497–8668* ⊘ *Closed Sun. and Sept. mid Oct. No lunch.*

★ Elvis' Beach Bar

$$ | **MODERN AMERICAN** | One of the most famous beach restaurants in the Caribbean, Elvis' is a hub of nightlife on the island, catering to all kinds of visitors and Hollywood A-listers. The bar is actually a boat; you can sit around it or with your feet in the sand under umbrella-covered tables on the beach. **Known for:** big screen TVs with sports on; Mexican food and potent drinks; the famous Goatchos and goat taco. $ *Average main: $20* ✉ *Northern End, Sandy Ground beach* ☎ *264/476–0101* ⊕ *www.elvisbeachbar.com.*

★ Hibernia Restaurant and Art Gallery

$$$$ | **ECLECTIC** | Creative dishes are served in this wood-beam cottage restaurant overlooking the water at Anguilla's eastern end. The tables in the intimate dining room face a Balinese-style pool with a fountain, sure to inspire relaxation during dinner. **Known for:** can't-miss smoked Caribbean fish appetizer; white chocolate and lavender ice cream meringue cake; eclectic dining. $ *Average main: $36* ✉ *Harbor Ridge Dr., Island Harbour* ☎ *264/497–4290* ⊕ *www.hiberniarestaurant.com* ⊘ *Closed Sun. and Mon. and from Aug.–Oct.; no lunch except Tues. and Fri.*

★ Jacala Beach Restaurant

$$$ | **FRENCH** | On beautiful Meads Bay, this restaurant continues to receive raves. Chef Alain has created a lovely open-air restaurant that turns out carefully prepared and nicely presented French food accompanied by good wines and personal attention. **Known for:** friendly beachside service; filet mignon cooked to perfection; best-in-the-Caribbean reputation. $ *Average main: $38* ✉ *Meads Bay Beach, Long Bay Village* ☎ *264/498–5888* ⊕ *www.facebook.com/jacala-beach-restaurant* ⊘ *Closed Mon. and Tues. and Aug.–Sept.*

Johnno's Beach Stop

$$ | CARIBBEAN | FAMILY | Now operating at lunch on Thursday to Sunday, Johnno's offers some of the best seafood on the island. Enjoy succulent fried, boiled, or steamed fish with sides like rice and peas, French fries or funchi (a hearty polenta). **Known for:** seafood; classic Caribbean beach bar; outpost on Prickly Pear Cay. $ *Average main: $20 ⊠ Sandy Ground, Sandy Ground Village ☎ 264/497–2728 ⊕ www.facebook.com/johnnosbeachstop ⊘ Closed Mon.–Wed. No dinner.*

Leon's at Meads Bay

$$ | ECLECTIC | Part of the neighboring Malliouhana Resort, this trendy beach shack has a local, laid-back atmosphere. Have lunch on the colorful benches or sit in comfortable lounge chaises under bright umbrellas while you enjoy johnnycake burgers, ceviche, and crispy snacks. **Known for:** toes-in-the-sand dining; great sunset spot; live music on weekends. $ *Average main: $15 ⊠ Malliouhana Resort, Meads Bay, West End Village ☎ 264/497–6117 ⊕ aubergeresorts.com/malliouhana/dine/leons-meads-bay ⊘ Closed Mon. and Tues.*

Madeariman Bar and Restaurant

$$$ | BRASSERIE | FAMILY | This casual, feet-in-the-sand bistro right on beautiful Shoal Bay East is open for breakfast, lunch, and dinner. The soups, salads, and simple grills here are served in generous portions with a bit of French flair, and the delicious pizzas are cooked in a stone oven. **Known for:** great stone oven pizza; simple yet tasty food; prime location on Shoal Bay East. $ *Average main: $26 ⊠ Shoal Bay East, Shoal Bay Village ☎ 264/497–5750 ⊕ www.madeariman.restaurant.*

Mango's Seaside Grill

$$$$ | SEAFOOD | FAMILY | Sparkling-fresh fish specialties have starring roles here. Sit in this semi-open-air restaurant on beautiful Barnes Bay and enjoy the salty breeze and sounds of the waves rolling in as you dive into light and healthy dishes like spicy grilled whole snapper and Cruzan rum–barbecued chicken. **Known for:** fresh fish dishes; mango ginger crème brulee; laid-back but high-end atmosphere. $ *Average main: $36 ⊠ Barnes Bay ☎ 264/497–6479 ⊕ www.mangosseasidegrill.com ⊘ Closed Tues. and Aug.–Oct.*

Ocean Echo

$$$$ | CARIBBEAN | FAMILY | It's nonstop every day from lunch until late at this relaxed and friendly restaurant, great for salads, burgers, grills, pasta, and fresh fish. A couple of times a week there is live music as well as the possibility of dancing with an excellent

island cocktail in hand. **Known for:** delicious pizzas and lobster salad; beachside tables; the "Rumzie," Anguilla's rum punch. ⑤ *Average main: $35* ✉ *Meads Bay Beach, Long Bay Village* ☎ *264/498–5454* ⊕ *www.oceanechoanguilla.com.*

Picante

$$$ | **MEXICAN** | **FAMILY** | This casual, wildly popular bright-red roadside Caribbean *taquería*, opened by a young California couple, serves huge, tasty burritos with a choice of fillings, fresh warm tortilla chips with first-rate guacamole, huge (and fresh) taco salads, seafood enchiladas, chipotle ribs, and tequila-lime chicken grilled under a brick. Passion-fruit margaritas are a must, and there are some serious tequila options. **Known for:** tacos; picnic-table seating; passion-fruit margarita. ⑤ *Average main: $21* ✉ *West End Rd., West End Village* ☎ *264/498–1616* ⊕ *www.picante-restaurant-anguilla.com* ⊙ *Closed Sun. and mid-Aug.–mid Oct. No lunch.*

Roy's Bayside Grill

$$$ | **CARIBBEAN** | **FAMILY** | Roy's is comfort food heaven, whether you crave red snapper fish-and-chips or a hamburger with all the fixings. Come any time of day for good cooking and a friendly vibe. **Known for:** incredible beachfront location; grilled lobster; home-style cooking and awesome margaritas. ⑤ *Average main: $25* ✉ *Road Bay, Sandy Ground Village* ☎ *264/497–2470* ⊕ *www.roysbaysidegrill.com.*

SandBar

$$ | **ECLECTIC** | Tasty and shareable small plates, a friendly beach vibe, and gorgeous sunsets are on offer here, as are cool music, gentle prices, and potent tropical cocktails. The menu changes seasonally, but it always features tapas brought to a new level, usually traditional foods prepared in unconventional ways. **Known for:** great sunset views; daily happy hour; big tapas plates at reasonable prices. ⑤ *Average main: $12* ✉ *Sandy Ground Village* ☎ *264/498–0171* ⊙ *Closed Sun. and Mon.*

Sharky's

$$$ | **CARIBBEAN** | **FAMILY** | A not-to-be-missed restaurant where Caribbean flavors steal the show, Sharky's is a result of Chef Lowell Hodge's perfectionism. He does a few things here and does them well, as a usually full house well attests ("house," by the way, is an operative word—you'll dine on the front porch of a private home). **Known for:** high-end dining for a fraction of the price; few menu items but all are hits; the chef's family recipes. ⑤ *Average main: $25* ✉ *Rte. 1 West End Village and Albert Hughes Dr.* ✛ *Just past the gas station* ☎ *264/729–0059* ▭ *No credit cards.*

★ Straw Hat

$$$$ | ECLECTIC | FAMILY | A charming owner, a gorgeous oceanfront location, sophisticated and original food, and friendly service are why this stylish restaurant on the beautiful Meads Bay has been in business since the mid-1990s. Whether for breakfast, lunch, late afternoon snack, or dinner, you will find appealing, tasty, and fresh choices to mix up or share. **Known for:** mahimahi and shrimp ceviche with plantain chips; fairly priced cocktails; beach view. ⑤ *Average main: $35* ⊠ *Frangipani Beach Resort, Long Bay Village* ☎ *264/497–8300* ⊕ *www.strawhat.com* ⊗ *Closed Sept. and Oct.*

Tasty's

$$$ | CARIBBEAN | FAMILY | Satisfying everyone's taste buds since 1999, this roadside restaurant in South Hill is a well-known spot for locals and visitors alike. You'll find that breakfast, lunch, tapas, or dinner at Tasty's is, well, very tasty. **Known for:** Tuesday and Friday happy hour; seafood salad; classic Caribbean with a creole edge. ⑤ *Average main: $26* ⊠ *Main Rd., South Hill Village* ☎ *264/584–2737* ⊕ *www.facebook.com/tastysrestaurantanguilla* ⊗ *Closed Thurs.*

Trattoria Tramonto Restaurant

$ | ITALIAN | FAMILY | The island's beloved beachfront Italian restaurant (open for lunch only) features a serenade of soft jazz on the sound system and gently lapping waves a few feet away. Pastas are homemade and served in a dozen ways. **Known for:** relaxing tropical ambience; beachy setting; classic Northern Italian meals next to the sea. ⑤ *Average main: $5* ⊠ *1254 Shoal Bay West, Shoal Bay Village* ☎ *264/497–8819* ⊕ *www.trattoriatramonto.com* ⊗ *Closed Mon. and Tues. and Aug.–Oct. No dinner.*

★ Veya and Meze at Veya

$$$$ | ECLECTIC | On the suavely minimalist four-sided verandah, stylishly appointed tables glow with flickering candlelight from sea urchin–shape porcelain votive holders. Chic patrons mingle and sip mojitos to the purr of soft jazz in a lively lounge. **Known for:** Moroccan shrimp "cigars"; live music nightly; Veya sparklers. ⑤ *Average main: $45* ⊠ *Sandy Ground Village* ☎ *264/498–8392* ⊕ *www.veyarestaurant.com* ⊗ *Closed Sun. and Sept.–mid-Oct. Closed Sat. in June–Aug. and in late Oct. No lunch.*

Hotels

Tourism on Anguilla is newer than some Caribbean islands—most development didn't begin until the early 1980s. The lack of native topography and, indeed, vegetation, and the blindingly white expanses of beach have inspired building designs of some interest; architecture buffs might have fun trying to name some of the most surprising examples. Inspiration largely comes from the Mediterranean: the Greek Islands, Morocco, and Spain, with some Miami-style art deco thrown into the mixture.

Anguilla accommodations basically fall into two categories: grand resorts and luxury resort-villas, or low-key, simple, locally owned apartments and small beachfront complexes. The former can be surprisingly expensive, the latter surprisingly reasonable. In the middle are some condo-type options, with full kitchens and multiple bedrooms, which are great for families or for longer stays. Private villa rentals are becoming more common and are increasing in number and quality of design and upkeep every season as development on the island accelerates.

A good phone chat or email exchange with the management of any property is a good idea, as units within the same complex can vary greatly in layout, accessibility, distance to the beach, and view. When calling to reserve a room, ask about special discount packages, especially in spring and summer. Most hotels include continental breakfast in the price, and many have meal-plan options. But keep in mind that Anguilla is home to dozens of excellent restaurants before you lock yourself into an expensive meal plan that you may not be able to change. All hotels charge a 10% tax, a $1 per room/per day tourism marketing levy, and—in most cases—an additional 10% service charge. A few properties include these charges in the published rates, so check carefully when evaluating prices.

PRIVATE VILLAS AND CONDOS

The tourist office publishes an annual *Anguilla Travel Planner* with informative listings of available vacation apartment rentals.

RENTAL CONTACTS

Ani Private Resorts

✉ *Little Bay* ☎ *718/577–1188* ⊕ *www.aniprivateresorts.com.*

Kishti Villa Collection

✉ *Long Bay Village* ☎ *609/225-5678, 264/235–2110* ⊕ *www. villakishticollection.com.*

HOTELS AND RESORTS

Altamer

$$$$ | RESORT | FAMILY | Architect Myron Goldfinger's geometric symphony of floor-to-ceiling windows, cantilevered walls, and curvaceous floating staircases set on a white-sand private beach is fit for any celebrity (or CEO)—as is the price tag. **Pros:** stunning decor and beautiful architectural design; outstanding luxury, privacy, and service; great for big groups. **Cons:** expensive; a minimum of 5 nights is required; a bit out of the way. $ *Rooms from: $4800* ✉ *Rte. 1, Shoal Bay Village* ☎ *800/475–9233* ⊕ *www. altamer.com* 🛏 *3 villas* ⦿ *Free Breakfast.*

Anguilla Great House Beach Resort

$$ | RESORT | FAMILY | These traditional West Indian–style bungalows are strung along one of Anguilla's longest beaches. **Pros:** real, old-school Caribbean; right on one of the most popular beaches; good prices. **Cons:** looks a bit tired; not exquisite or luxurious, which many seek in Anguilla; very simple rooms. $ *Rooms from: $310* ✉ *Rendezvous Bay* ☎ *264/497–6061, 800/583–9247* ⊕ *www. anguillagreathouse.com* 🛏 *31 rooms* ⦿ *No Meals.*

Aurora Anguilla Resort & Golf Club

$$$$ | RESORT | FAMILY | Formerly the Resorts and Residences by CuisinArt, this new and quite lavish resort operated by Olympus Ventures opened in late 2021. **Pros:** gorgeous, luxurious rooms; on-site restaurants, bars, and spa; Greg Norman golf course. **Cons:** beach can be rough; takes time to go to one end of the resort to the next; expensive. $ *Rooms from: $701* ✉ *Rendezvous Bay* ☎ *800/210–6444 U.S., 264/498–2000* ⊕ *www.auroraanguilla.com* 🛏 *98 rooms* ⦿ *Free Breakfast.*

★ Belmond Cap Juluca

$$$$ | RESORT | FAMILY | Strung along 179 acres of breathtaking Maundays Bay, these romantic, domed villas are a long-time Anguilla favorite, thanks to a caring staff, great sports facilities, and plenty of privacy and comfort. **Pros:** miles of talcum-soft sand; impeccable, warm service; great on-site restaurants. **Cons:** sun sets on the opposite side of the resort; comparatively high rates; may be booked well in advance. $ *Rooms from: $875* ✉ *Maunday's Bay* ☎ *264/497–6666, 264/497–6779 reservations* ⊕ *www. belmond.com/capjuluca* 🛏 *108 rooms* ⦿ *Free Breakfast.*

Carimar Beach Club

$$$$ | APARTMENT | FAMILY | This horseshoe of bougainvillea-draped Mediterranean-style buildings on beautiful Meads Bay has the look of a Sun Belt condo. **Pros:** great value; easy walk to restaurants and spa; excellent beach location. **Cons:** air-conditioning only in bedrooms; not much privacy in the courtyard; no pool or restaurant. $ *Rooms from: $480* ✉ *Meads Bay, West End Village* ☎ *264/497–6881, 800/681–6956 US* ⊕ *www.carimar.com* 🛏 *24 apartments* ⦿ *No Meals.*

★ Four Seasons Resort and Residences Anguilla

$$$$ | RESORT | FAMILY | On a promontory over 3,200 feet of pearly sand on Barnes Bay, this showpiece wows sophisticates. **Pros:**

state-of-the-art luxury; cutting-edge contemporary design; spacious rooms. **Cons:** very large resort; expensive; international rather than Caribbean feel. $ *Rooms from: $925* ⊠ *Barnes Bay, West End Village* ☎ *264/201–9580 US, 264800/497–7000* ⊕ *www. fourseasons.com/anguilla* ☉ *Closed end of Aug.–mid-Oct.* ⇌ *180 units* ⦿ *No Meals.*

Frangipani Beach Resort

$$$ | RESORT | FAMILY | Located on the beautiful Champagne sands of Meads Bay, this Mediterranean-style property has a welcoming and laid-back feel, and the friendly service immediately sets you at ease. **Pros:** great beach; good location for restaurant-hopping and water sports activities; first-rate on-site restaurant. **Cons:** more like a condo than a resort; you will not want to leave; some rooms lack a view. $ *Rooms from: $450* ⊠ *Meads Bay, West End Village* ☎ *264/497–6442* ⊕ *www.frangipaniresort.com* ☉ *Closed Sept. and Oct.* ⇌ *23 rooms* ⦿ *Free Breakfast.*

★ Malliouhana, An Auberge Resort

$$$$ | RESORT | This classic luxury hotel perched cliffside over beautiful Meads Bay beach is a fancifully modern yet relaxed beach paradise. **Pros:** great location on Meads Bay; friendly and attentive service; spacious rooms and bathrooms. **Cons:** property takes a fair amount of walking to get around; car necessary to explore the island (if you want to); lots of stairs and no elevators. $ *Rooms from: $1399* ⊠ *Meads Bay* ☎ *264/497–6111* ⊕ *aubergeresorts. com/malliouhana* ☉ *Closed late Aug.–late Oct.* ⇌ *58 rooms* ⦿ *No Meals.*

Meads Bay Beach Villas

$$$$ | APARTMENT | FAMILY | These gorgeous one-, two-, and three-bedroom villas right on Meads Bay have a cult following, so it can be hard to book them, but if you score a stay here, you'll understand why. **Pros:** large private villas; beautiful beach; private pools. **Cons:** very busy resort but service still remains excellent; if you like complaining, you may get bored—this is a top-notch resort; more condo than hotel in terms of service. $ *Rooms from: $700* ⊠ *Meads Bay Rd., West End Village* ☎ *215/550–6011 Ext. 105 US, 264/497–0273* ⊕ *www.meadsbaybeachvillas.com* ⇌ *4 villas* ⦿ *No Meals.*

Quintessence

$$$$ | HOTEL | Walking into this 5-star Relais & Chateaux hotel is like walking into a grand mansion, with a main reception area that can only be described as a tropical gallery; the owner's collection of Haitian art is the biggest outside of Haiti. **Pros:** intimate and private; superb service; excellent on-site dining experiences. **Cons:**

beach is a steep walk downhill and there are no elevators; only 9 suites; no kids under 12 years old. $ *Rooms from: $1250* ✉ *Long Bay, Long Bay Village* ☎ *800/234–7468 US Toll Free, 264/498–8106* ⊕ *www.qhotelanguilla.com* ⇥ *9 suites* |◉| *No Meals.*

Serenity Cottages

$$ | **APARTMENT** | **FAMILY** | Despite the name, these aren't cottages but large, fully equipped, and relatively affordable one- and two-bedroom apartments (and studios) in a small complex set in a lush garden at the far end of glorious Shoal Bay Beach East. **Pros:** quiet end of beach with snorkeling outside the door; weeklong packages; two convenient restaurants. **Cons:** more condo than hotel in terms of staff; location requires a car and extra time to drive to the West End; no pool. $ *Rooms from: $350* ✉ *Shoal Bay Village* ☎ *264/497–3328* ⊕ *www.serenity.ai* ☾ *Closed Sept.* ⇥ *10 units* |◉| *No Meals.*

Shoal Bay Villas

$$$ | **APARTMENT** | **FAMILY** | In this old-style property on Shoal Bay's incredible 2-mile (3-km) beach, studios and one- and two-bedroom apartments all have balconies over the water. **Pros:** friendly and casual beachfront property; full kitchens; pool and spa on-site. **Cons:** you'll want a car; luxury touches are lacking; rather basic. $ *Rooms from: $420* ✉ *Shoal Bay Village* ☎ *562/366-4813 VOIP, 264/497–2051* ⊕ *www.sbvillas.ai* ☾ *Closed Aug. 30–Oct. 24* ⇥ *12 units* |◉| *No Meals.*

★ Tranquility Beach

$$$$ | **RESORT** | With modern one-, two- or three-bedroom condos right on beautiful Meads Bay, this resort, completed in 2020, is one of the island's newest luxury beachfront experiences. **Pros:** friendly and dedicated staff; excellent beach service; private hot tub. **Cons:** feels more like a condominium than a resort; no swimming pool; breakfast not included in the rate. $ *Rooms from: $575* ✉ *Meads Bay, West End Village* ☎ *264/462–6000* ⊕ *www. tranquilitybeachanguilla.com* ⇥ *15 condos* |◉| *No Meals.*

Turtle's Nest Beach Resort

$$ | **APARTMENT** | **FAMILY** | This complex of studios and one- to three-bedroom oceanfront condos is right on Meads Bay Beach, with some of the island's best restaurants a sandy stroll away. **Pros:** beachfront; huge apartments; well-kept grounds and pool. **Cons:** may need a car if you want to explore; may be busy in high season; no elevator, so fourth-floor units are a climb (but have great views). $ *Rooms from: $375* ✉ *Meads Bay, West End Village* ☎ *264/476–7979, 264/497–7979* ⊕ *www.turtlesnestanguilla. com* ⇥ *22 units* |◉| *No Meals.*

Zemi Beach House Hotel & Spa / Residences

$$$$ | **RESORT** | With two pools, two restaurants, a Rhum Room for cocktails and cigars, a tennis court, and a kids' program, there's something for everyone at this luxury resort on a gorgeous, 400-foot stretch of Shoal Bay East's white-sand beach. **Pros:** fabulous beach location; desirable amenities; beautiful boutique property. **Cons:** expensive; during busiest weeks restaurant service may be less than perfect; need a car to get around the island. $ *Rooms from: $695* ⊠ *Shoal Bay Village* ☎ *264/584–0001* ⊕ *www.zemibeach.com* ➳ *76 rooms* ❄ *No Meals.*

Nightlife

In mid- to late March, on the first full moon before Easter, reggae star and impresario Bankie Banx stages Moonsplash, a three-day music festival that showcases local and imported talent. Anguilla Day's boat races, in May, are the most important sporting event of the year. At the end of July, the Anguilla Summer Festival has boat races by day and Carnival parades, calypso competitions, and parties at night. Some years bring a jazz festival.

Most hotels and many restaurants offer live entertainment in high season and on weekends: it might include pianists, jazz combos, or traditional steel and calypso bands. Friday and Saturday, Sandy Ground is the hot spot; Wednesday and Sunday the action shifts to Shoal Bay.

Nightlife action doesn't really start until 9 and runs late into the night. Be aware that taxis are not readily available then. If you plan to take a cab back to your lodging at the end of the night, make arrangements in advance with the driver who brings you to your destination or with your hotel concierge.

Dune Preserve

LIVE MUSIC | There is live music on Wednesday, Friday, and Sunday nights at this funky driftwood-fabricated home of reggae star Bankie Banx, who often performs here. By day it's the quintessential beach bar with barbecue ribs and grilled fresh seafood. At night there's a dance floor, beach bar, small menu, and potent rum cocktails, of course. In high season there's a $20 cover. Moonsplash, an annual three-day event in March, is not to be missed. ⊠ *Rendezvous Bay* ☎ *264/729–4215* ⊕ *www.bankiebanx.net/dunepreserve.*

★ Elvis' Beach Bar

BARS | Actually a boat, this popular beach bar is a great place to hear music and sip the best rum punch on Earth. You can also snack on Mexican food (try the goat tacos), play beach volleyball, or watch any happening sports event on the big TV. The bar is closed Tuesday, and there's live music occasionally. The sunsets here are spectacular and always mark the beginning of another great night. ✉ *Sandy Ground Village* ☎ *264/498–0101* ⊕ *www. elvisbeachbar.com.*

Shopping

ART AND CRAFTS

★ Anguilla Sands and Salts

CRAFTS | Gorgeous jewelry, unique souvenirs, bath salts, body scrubs, and infused sea salt are handmade with resources found in Anguilla at this charming local shop. Jewelry created with sand from the island's beaches allows you to take a piece of your favorite beach with you, while salt gathered from the island's salt ponds by the owner himself forms the salt products. The sea salts are infused with herbs like rosemary, thyme, onion, garlic, and curry. Fun themed nights include Margarita Thursday, when the back patio transforms into a hangout for locals and visitors and margaritas are served (in sea salt–rimmed glasses, of course). ✉ *South Hill, South Hill Village* ☎ *264/582–9211* ⊕ *www.anguilla-sands.com.*

Boutique Bijoux

JEWELRY & WATCHES | It's almost impossible to leave without buying something at this cute store in Sandy Ground; it's the place for fun handmade sterling silver jewelry, fabulous hand bags and totes, cover-ups, and handmade souvenirs. ✉ *Sandy Ground, Sandy Ground Village* ☎ *264/583–0823* ⊕ *www.facebook.com/anguilla.bijoux* ⊙ *Closed Sun.*

Devonish Art Gallery

CRAFTS | This gallery purveys the wood, stone, and clay creations of Courtney Devonish, an internationally known potter and sculptor, plus creations by his wife, Carolle, a bead artist. Works by other Caribbean artists and regional antique maps are also available. ✉ *Lower South Hill, South Hill Village* ☎ *264/584–6019* ⊕ *www.devonishart.com.*

Hibernia Restaurant and Art Gallery

ART GALLERIES | Striking pieces are culled from the owners' travels, from contemporary Eastern European art to traditional Southeast Asian crafts. The gallery is accessible during restaurant opening hours or by appointment. ✉ *Harbor Ridge Dr., Island Harbour* ☎ *264/497–4290* ⊕ *www.hiberniarestaurant.com* ⊙ *Closed Sun. and Mon. and Aug.–Oct.*

L. Bernbaum Art Gallery

ART GALLERIES | Originally from Texas, Lynne Bernbaum has been working and living in the Caribbean for decades and exhibits around the world. Her paintings and prints are inspired by the island's natural beauty but have unusual perspectives and a hint of surrealism. The gallery is open Wednesday through Saturday 11–5 pm. ⊠ *Sandy Ground Village* ☎ *264/476–5211* ⊕ *www.lynnebernbaum.com.*

Paint Studios

ART GALLERIES | FAMILY | This delightful gallery and art studio in Shoal Bay East not only offers beautiful pieces by local artists but also spectacular views of the turquoise waters of one of the island's best beaches. Owned and operated by Anguilla resident and artist Emily Garlick, Paint is much more than just a place where art is exhibited. There are four resident artists that use the space to work, allowing you to be a part of their creative process. Next to art events and exhibits, this studio also hosts paint classes for kids and adults, including their popular "Sip and Paint" events. ⊠ *Shoal Bay East, Shoal Bay Village* ☎ *264/772–3652.*

CLOTHING

Irie Life

CRAFTS | This popular boutique sells vividly hued beach and resort wear and flip-flops, as well as attractive handicrafts, jewelry, and collectibles from all over the Caribbean. ⊠ *South Hill Village* ☎ *264/497–6527* ⊕ *www.irielife.com.*

Limin' Boutique

JEWELRY & WATCHES | Visit this attractive boutique for sensational repurposed jewelry and handicrafts such as bags and totes made from old sails from Anguilla's famous racing boats, "Dune Jewelry" made from the sand from local beaches, hand-designed purses, and Mela jewelry made from natural elements found on the island. There is also a good selection of stylish beach cover-ups and hand-painted Christmas ornaments. ⊠ *Tranquility Beach Resort, John Hodge Dr., Meads Bay, West End Village* ☎ *264/583–3733* ⊕ *www.liminartisangifting.com* ☉ *Closed Sun.*

Petals Boutique

JEWELRY & WATCHES | This lovely boutique has attractive beachwear, jewelry, and accessories, as well as an assortment of local products. ⊠ *Frangipani Beach Resort, Rte. 1, Long Bay Village* ☎ *264/497–6442* ☉ *Closed Mon.*

SeaSpray Boutique and Smoothies

CRAFTS | Enjoy a rum punch or a delicious fruit smoothie while you shop for Anguillian arts and crafts, handcrafted jewelry, and charming handmade Christmas ornaments. They stock delicious locally made preserves from Anguilla's Jammin, locally made banana rum, and souvenirs. ⊠ *South Hill Roundabout, The Valley* ☎ *264/235–1650* ⊕ *www.facebook.com/SeaSprayAnguilla* ⊘ *Closed Sun.*

FOOD AND WINE
Grands Vins de France
WINE/SPIRITS | The best vino on Anguilla can be found in this wine shop in South Hill. Wine aficionados will not be disappointed by the magnificent 1,300-deep collection. Wines not only from France but also from the U.S., Argentina, Italy, New Zealand, South Africa, and Spain are for sale and range from $8 to $3,000 per bottle. An expert wine consultant can assist you with choosing the right wine. ⊠ *South Hill, South Hill Village* ☎ *264/497–6498, 264/235–6498* ⊕ *facebook.com/grandsvinsdefranceanguilla.*

🏃 Activities

Anguilla's expanding sports options include an excellent golf course (at the Aurora Golf Resort), designed by Greg Norman to accentuate the natural terrain and maximize the stunning ocean views over Rendezvous Bay. Players say the par-72 course is reminiscent of Pebble Beach. Guided tours are also an option; a round-the-island tour by taxi takes about 2½ hours and costs about $80 for one or two people, $10 for each additional passenger. Special-interest nature and culture tours are available.

DIVING
Anguilla boasts seven marine parks; sunken wrecks; a long barrier reef; walls, canyons, and hulking boulders; varied marine life, including greenback turtles and nurse sharks; and exceptionally clear water. All make for excellent diving. **Prickly Pear Cay** is a favorite spot. **Stoney Bay Marine Park,** off the northeast end, showcases the *El Buen Consejo,* a 960-ton Spanish galleon that sank in 1772. Divers love finding all 29 cannons. Other good dive sites include **Grouper Bowl,** with exceptional hard-coral formations; **Ram's Head,** with caves, chutes, and tunnels; and **Upper Flats,** where you are sure to see stingrays.

★ SCUBA SHACK - Shoal Bay Scuba and Watersports
BOATING | **FAMILY** | This highly rated PADI dive center runs daily private dives and scheduled dives for certified divers Monday through Friday from Roy's Bayside Grill in Sandy Ground. Dives with full equipment start at $180. Advanced courses, snorkeling, and sightseeing trips are also available. There's a full range of PADI courses for adults and kids; the minimum age is 10 years old. The

A Day at the Boat Races

If you want a different kind of trip to Anguilla, try for a visit during Carnival, which usually starts on the first Monday in August and continues for about 10 days. Colorful parades, beauty pageants, music, delicious food, arts-and-crafts shows, fireworks, and nonstop partying are just the beginning. The music starts with sunrise jam sessions—as early as 4 am—and continues well into the night. The high point? The boat races. A national passion, it's the official national sport of Anguilla and the highlight of many other cultural events like Anguilla Day.

Anguillians from around the world return home to race old-fashioned, made-on-the-island wooden boats that have been in use on the island since the early 1800s. Similar to some of today's fastest sailboats, these are 15 to 28 feet in length and sport only a mainsail and jib on a single 25-foot mast. The sailboats have no deck, so heavy bags of sand, boulders, and sometimes even people are used as ballast. As the boats reach the finish line, the ballast—including some of the sailors—gets thrown into the water in a furious effort to win the race. Spectators line the beaches and follow the boats on foot, by car, and from even more boats. You'll have almost as much fun watching the fans as you will the races.

shop sells masks, snorkels, fins, T-shirts, hats, and shirts. You can find availability and complete scheduling, secure booking, the liability release, and certification cards on their website. ⊠ *Roy's Bayside Grill, Sandy Ground Village* ☎ *264/235–1482* ⊕ *www. scubashackaxa.com* ☞ *Booking and liability releases via website.*

GOLF

★ Aurora International Golf Club

GOLF | This Greg Norman course, renovated when it became part of Aurora Anguilla Resort & Golf Club, qualifies as one of the best golf courses in the Caribbean. Thirteen of its 18 holes are directly on the water, and it features sweeping sea vistas, elevation changes, and an ecologically responsible watering system of ponds and lagoons that snake through the grounds. Players including President Bill Clinton have thrilled to the spectacular vistas of St. Martin and blue sea at the tee box of the 390-yard starting hole—the Caribbean's answer to Pebble Beach. There's also a 9-hole short course. ⊠ *Aurora Anguilla Resort & Golf Club, Rendezvous Bay* ☎ *800/210–6444* ⊕ *auroraanguilla.com/golf* ⊠ *$395 for 18 holes ($245 resort guests), $295 for 9 holes ($185 hotel guests)* ⅄ *18 holes, 7200 yards, par 72.*

HORSEBACK RIDING
Seaside Stables
HORSEBACK RIDING | FAMILY | Ever dreamed of a sunset gallop (or slow clomp) on the beach? A private ocean ride in the morning or afternoon is $125 for 60 to 75 minutes. Prior riding experience is not required as the horses are very gentle. Choose from English or Western saddles. ✉ *Paradise Dr., Cove Bay* ☎ *264/235–3667* ⊕ *www.seasidestablesanguilla.com* ✉ *$125 per ride* ☞ *No group rides.*

SEA EXCURSIONS
A number of boating options are available for airport transfers, day trips to offshore cays, day trips to St. Martin and St. Barth, or just whipping through the waves en route to a picnic spot.

Calypso Charters
BOATING | FAMILY | Book a private or semiprivate charter with Calypso on one of their eight powerboats for a trip around Anguilla, a deep-sea fishing trip, or a sea excursion to neighboring islands St. Barth and St. Martin. They offer a lovely two-hour sunset cruise leaving from Sandy Ground and you can book your airport transfer, private or otherwise, with them as well. Their local captains are some of the most experienced and know the waters around Anguilla well. ✉ *Sandy Ground Village* ☎ *264/584–8504, 264/462–8504* ⊕ *www.calypsochartersanguilla.com* ✉ *Airport transfer: $65 per adult one-way.*

Funtime Charters
BOATING | With 11 powerboats from 32 to 48 feet, this charter and shuttle service arranges private and scheduled boat transport to the airport, including luggage services ($70 per person one way for adults); day trips to St. Barth; and other powerboat excursions, including inter-island excursions. ✉ *West End Village* ☎ *264/497–6511* ⊕ *www.funtimecharters.com.*

★ Junior's Glass Bottom Boat
DIVING & SNORKELING | FAMILY | Junior has a great reputation for showing you the underwater scenery of Anguilla, starting with reef trips on his glass-bottom boat. For an underwater peek at sea turtles and stingrays without getting wet, catch a ride with him. Guided snorkeling trips and instruction are available, too; Junior is great with kids and very knowledgeable. It's best to book in advance, especially during holidays. His services are $40 per person per hour or $80 per person per hour with snorkeling included; children 5 years and under are free. ✉ *Shoal Bay Village* ☎ *264/235–1008* ⊕ *www.junior.ai.*

★ **Sandy Island**

BOATING | FAMILY | Spend the day swimming, lounging, eating, and snorkeling on this breathtaking cay off Sandy Ground. This tiny spit of sand is famous for its beach bar, serving local seafood and fresh fruit cocktails. They also have a great wine list and a stunning view. Take the daily sea shuttle, appropriately called *Happiness,* from the small pier in Sandy Ground to this oasis in the middle of the ocean for about $40 round-trip or book a private day trip with one of the many charter boat companies that have Sandy Island as part of their itinerary. ⊠ *Sandy Ground Village* ☎ *264/497–6534* ⊕ *www.mysandyisland.com* ☞ *Open by reservation only Sept. 1–Oct. 31.*

Surf AXA

SURFING | Surf AXA offers everything for beginner or experienced surfers, including instruction and surfboard rentals. Guided surf tours are also available here, as well as ECO land tours. Operating out of the colorful Lime Keel House in East End, which offers a Saturday dinner and a Sunday Brunch, this spot is a must for surfers, wanna-be surfers, and nature lovers. ⊠ *South Hill Village* ☎ *264/583–4613* ⊕ *surfaxa.com* ✉ *$20 board rental, $250 off shore surf tour, $80 surf lesson and $100 ECO tours* ☞ *Book via website.*

Index

Photo Credits